EDWIN ARLINGTON ROBINSON

Modern Critical Views

Chinua Achebe
Henry Adams
Aeschylus
S. Y. Agnon
Edward Albee
Raphael Alberti
Louisa May Alcott
A. R. Ammons
Sherwood Anderson
Aristophanes
Matthew Arnold
Antonin Artaud
John Ashbery
Margaret Atwood
W. H. Auden
Jane Austen
Isaac Babel
Sir Francis Bacon
James Baldwin
Honoré de Balzac
John Barth
Donald Barthelme
Charles Baudelaire
Simone de Beauvoir
Samuel Beckett
Saul Bellow
Thomas Berger
John Berryman
The Bible
Elizabeth Bishop
William Blake
Giovanni Boccaccio
Heinrich Böll
Jorge Luis Borges
Elizabeth Bowen
Bertolt Brecht
The Brontës
Charles Brockden Brown
Sterling Brown
Robert Browning
Martin Buber
John Bunyan
Anthony Burgess
Kenneth Burke
Robert Burns
William Burroughs
George Gordon, Lord
  Byron
Pedro Calderón de la Barca
Italo Calvino
Albert Camus
Canadian Poetry: Modern
  and Contemporary
Canadian Poetry through
  E. J. Pratt
Thomas Carlyle
Alejo Carpentier
Lewis Carroll
Willa Cather
Louis-Ferdinand Céline
Miguel de Cervantes

Geoffrey Chaucer
John Cheever
Anton Chekhov
Kate Chopin
Chrétien de Troyes
Agatha Christie
Samuel Taylor Coleridge
Colette
William Congreve & the
  Restoration Dramatists
Joseph Conrad
Contemporary Poets
James Fenimore Cooper
Pierre Corneille
Julio Cortázar
Hart Crane
Stephen Crane
e. e. cummings
Dante
Robertson Davies
Daniel Defoe
Philip K. Dick
Charles Dickens
James Dickey
Emily Dickinson
Denis Diderot
Isak Dinesen
E. L. Doctorow
John Donne & the
  Seventeenth-Century
  Metaphysical Poets
John Dos Passos
Fyodor Dostoevsky
Frederick Douglass
Theodore Dreiser
John Dryden
W. E. B. Du Bois
Lawrence Durrell
George Eliot
T. S. Eliot
Elizabethan Dramatists
Ralph Ellison
Ralph Waldo Emerson
Euripides
William Faulkner
Henry Fielding
F. Scott Fitzgerald
Gustave Flaubert
E. M. Forster
John Fowles
Sigmund Freud
Robert Frost
Northrop Frye
Carlos Fuentes
William Gaddis
André Gide
W. S. Gilbert
Allen Ginsberg
J. W. von Goethe
Nikolai Gogol
William Golding

Oliver Goldsmith
Mary Gordon
Günther Grass
Robert Graves
Graham Greene
Thomas Hardy
Nathaniel Hawthorne
William Hazlitt
H. D.
Seamus Heaney
Lillian Hellman
Ernest Hemingway
Hermann Hesse
Geoffrey Hill
Friedrich Hölderlin
Homer
A. D. Hope
Gerard Manley Hopkins
Horace
A. E. Housman
William Dean Howells
Langston Hughes
Ted Hughes
Victor Hugo
Zora Neale Hurston
Aldous Huxley
Henrik Ibsen
Eugene Ionesco
Washington Irving
Henry James
Dr. Samuel Johnson and
  James Boswell
Ben Jonson
James Joyce
Carl Gustav Jung
Franz Kafka
Yasonari Kawabata
John Keats
Søren Kierkegaard
Rudyard Kipling
Melanie Klein
Heinrich von Kleist
Philip Larkin
D. H. Lawrence
John le Carré
Ursula K. Le Guin
Giacomo Leopardi
Doris Lessing
Sinclair Lewis
Jack London
Frederico García Lorca
Robert Lowell
Malcolm Lowry
Norman Mailer
Bernard Malamud
Stéphane Mallarmé
Thomas Malory
André Malraux
Thomas Mann
Katherine Mansfield
Christopher Marlowe

Continued at back of book

Modern Critical Views

EDWIN ARLINGTON ROBINSON

Edited and with an introduction by
Harold Bloom
Sterling Professor of the Humanities
Yale University

CHELSEA HOUSE PUBLISHERS ◇ 1988
New York ◇ New Haven ◇ Philadelphia

© 1988 by Chelsea House Publishers, a division
of Chelsea House Educational Communications, Inc.,
   95 Madison Avenue, New York, NY 10016
   345 Whitney Avenue, New Haven, CT 06511
   5068B West Chester Pike, Edgemont, PA 19028

Printed and bound in the United States of America

10   9   8   7   6   5   4   3   2   1

∝ The paper used in this publication meets the minimum
requirements of the American National Standard for
Permanence of Paper for Printed Library Materials, Z39.48-
1984.

Library of Congress Cataloging-in-Publication Data

Edwin Arlington Robinson.
   (Modern critical views)
   Bibliography: p.
   Includes index.
   Summary: A collection of nine critical essays
discussing the American poet, arranged in chronological
order of their original publication.
   1. Robinson, Edwin Arlington, 1869–1935—Criticism
and interpretation. [1. Robinson, Edwin Arlington,
1869–1935—Criticism and interpretation. 2. American
literature—History and criticism] I. Bloom, Harold.
II. Series.
PS3535.025Z652   1988   811'.52   87–10085
ISBN 1–55546–322–3 (alk. paper)

Contents

Editor's Note   vii

Introduction   1
   Harold Bloom

A Cool Master   5
   Yvor Winters

The Old Poetry and the New: Robinson   13
   Roy Harvey Pearce

A Poet of Continuing Relevance   29
   Denis Donoghue

Edwin Arlington Robinson: The Many Truths   55
   James Dickey

The Idealist *in Extremis*   73
   Hyatt H. Waggoner

The Transformation of Merlin   101
   Nathan Comfort Starr

A Grave and Solitary Voice   115
   Irving Howe

Robinson and the Years Ahead   127
   Josephine Miles

The Poetry of Edwin Arlington Robinson   137
   John Lucas

Chronology   155

Contributors   159

Contents

Editor's Note   vii

Introduction   1
   Harold Bloom

A Cool Master   5
   Yvor Winters

The Old Poetry and the New: Robinson   13
   Roy Harvey Pearce

A Poet of Continuing Relevance   29
   Denis Donoghue

Edwin Arlington Robinson: The Many Truths   55
   James Dickey

The Idealist *in Extremis*   73
   Hyatt H. Waggoner

The Transformation of Merlin   101
   Nathan Comfort Starr

A Grave and Solitary Voice   115
   Irving Howe

Robinson and the Years Ahead   127
   Josephine Miles

The Poetry of Edwin Arlington Robinson   137
   John Lucas

Chronology   155

Contributors   159

Bibliography 161

Acknowledgments 165

Index 167

Editor's Note

This book gathers together a representative collection of the best criticism devoted to the poetry of Edwin Arlington Robinson. The critical essays are reprinted here in the chronological order of their original publication. I am grateful to Neil Arditi for his aid in editing this book.

My introduction considers the early Robinson as an Emersonian poet, a Transcendentalist addicted to an asceticism of the spirit. The chronological sequence begins with Yvor Winters's review of Robinson's *Collected Poems,* a review that commends Robinson for having survived and carried on the tradition of Emerson and Dickinson.

Roy Harvey Pearce emphasizes Robinson's power at portraying failure, while lamenting Robinson's own failure as a philosophical poet. In a generous and informed estimate, Denis Donoghue compares Robinson's best shorter poems with Hardy's, while appreciating the American poet's deep need of the mythological aspects of his Arthurian poems.

The poet James Dickey, in a surprising tribute, commends Robinson for "answering little but asking those questions that are unpardonable, unforgettable, and necessary." A more Emersonian appreciation, by Hyatt H. Waggoner, rightly chronicles the influence of the severe, later Emerson upon Robinson, the idealist in extremis, or a Transcendentalist in the last ditch.

The long poem *Merlin* is analyzed by Nathan Comfort Starr as a poignant transformation of the traditional story into a tale of doomed love and of metaphysical disillusionment. Irving Howe, praising Robinson's grave and solitary voice, finds the lyricist of the shorter poems to be a crucial influence upon James Dickey, Robert Lowell, and James Wright.

The poet and critic Josephine Miles traces Robinson's relation to poetic tradition, while noting that "he praises with nostalgia and he blames with apprehension." In this book's final essay, John Lucas isolates Robinson's salient excellences as "plain realities," "surprises," and "an unfailing curiosity."

Introduction

Emerson himself was a product of New England and a man of strong moral habits. . . . He gave to American romanticism, in spite of its irresponsible doctrine, a religious tone which it has not yet lost and which has often proved disastrous . . . there is a good deal of this intellectual laziness in Robinson; and as a result of the laziness, there is a certain admixture of Emersonian doctrine, which runs counter to the principles governing most of his work and the best of it.

—YVOR WINTERS

The Torrent and the Night Before (published late in 1896 by Robinson himself) remains one of the best first volumes in our poetry. Three of its shorter poems—"George Crabbe," "Luke Havergal," "The Clerks"—Robinson hardly surpassed, and three more—"Credo," "Walt Whitman" (which Robinson unfortunately abandoned), and "The Children of the Night" (reprinted as title-poem in his next volume)—are memorable work, all in the earlier Emersonian mode that culminates in "Bacchus." The stronger "Luke Havergal" stems from the darker Emersonianism of "Experience" and "Fate," and has a relation to the singular principles of "Merlin." It prophesies Robinson's finest later lyrics, such as "Eros Turannos" and "For a Dead Lady," and suggests the affinity between Robinson and Frost that is due to their common Emersonian tradition.

In *Captain Craig* (1902) Robinson published "The Sage," a direct hymn of homage to Emerson, whose *The Conduct of Life* had moved him profoundly at a first reading in August 1899. Robinson had read the earlier Emerson well before, but it is fascinating that he came to essays like "Fate" and "Power" only after writing "Luke Havergal" and some similar poems, for his deeper nature then discovered itself anew. He called "Luke Haver-

1

gal" "a piece of deliberate degeneration," which I take to mean what an
early letter calls "sympathy for failure where fate has been abused and self
demoralized." Browning, the other great influence upon Robinson, is ob-
sessed with "deliberate degeneration" in this sense; Childe Roland's and
Andrea del Sarto's failures are wilful abuses of fate and demoralizations of
self. "The Sage" praises Emerson's "fierce wisdom," emphasizes Asia's influence upon him, and hardly touches his dialectical optimism. This Emerson
is "previsioned of the madness and the mean," fit seer for "the fiery night"
of "Luke Havergal":

> But there, where western glooms are gathering,
> The dark will end the dark, if anything:
> God slays Himself with every leaf that flies,
> And hell is more than half of paradise.

These are the laws of Compensation, "or that nothing is got for nothing," as Emerson says in "Power." At the depth of Robinson is this Emersonian fatalism, as it is in Frost, and even in Henry James. "The world is
mathematical," Emerson says, "and has no casualty in all its vast and flow-
ing curve." Robinson, brooding on the end of "Power," confessed: "He
really gets after one," and spoke of Emerson as walloping one "with a big
New England shingle," the cudgel of Fate. But Robinson was walloped too
well, by which I do not mean what Winters means, since I cannot locate
any "intellectual laziness" in Emerson. Unlike Browning and Hardy, Robinson yielded too much to Necessity, and too rapidly assimilated himself to
the tendency I have named Merlin. Circumstances and temperament share
in Robinson's obsession with Nemesis, but poetic misprision is part of the
story also, for Robinson's *tessera* in regard to Emerson relies on completing
the sage's fatalism. From Emerson's categories of power and circumstance,
Robinson fashions a more complete single category, in a personal idealism
that is a "philosophy of desperation," as he feared it might be called. The
persuasive desperation of "Luke Havergal" and "Eros Turannos" is his best
expression of this nameless idealism that is also a fatalism, but "The Children of the Night," for all its obtrusive echoes of Tennyson and even Longfellow, shows more clearly what Robinson found to be a possible stance:

> It is the crimson not the gray,
>   That charms the twilight of all time;
> It is the promise of the day
>   That makes the starry sky sublime;

It is the faith within the fear
That holds us to the life we curse;—
So let us in ourselves revere
The Self which is the Universe!

The bitter charm of this is that it qualifies so severely its too-hopeful and borrowed music. Even so early, Robinson has "completed" Emersonian Self-Reliance and made it his own by emphasizing its Stoic as against its transcendental or Bacchic aspect. When, in "Credo," Robinson feels "the coming glory of the Light!," the light nevertheless emanates from unaware angels who wove "dead leaves to garlands where no roses are." It is not that Robinson believed, with Melville, that the invisible spheres were formed in fright, but he shrewdly suspected that the ultimate world, though existent, was nearly as destitute as this one. He is an Emersonian incapable of transport, an ascetic of the transcendental spirit, contrary to an inspired saint like Jones Very or to the Emerson of "The Poet," but a contrary, not a negation, to use Blake's distinction. Not less gifted than Frost, he achieves so much less because he gave himself away to Necessity so soon in his poetic life. Frost's Job quotes "Uriel" to suggest that confusion is "the form of forms," the way all things return upon themselves, like rays:

Though I hold rays deteriorate to nothing,
First white, then red, then ultra red, then out.

This is cunning and deep in Frost, the conviction that "all things come round," even the mental confusions of God as He morally blunders. What we miss in Robinson is this quality of savagery, the strength that can end "Directive" by saying:

Here are your waters and your watering place.
Drink and be whole again beyond confusion.

To be beyond confusion is to be beyond the form of forms that is Fate's, and to be whole beyond Fate suggests an end to circlings, a resolution to all the Emersonian turnings that see unity, and yet behold divisions. Frost will play at being Merlin, many times, but his wariness saved him from Robinson's self-exhaustions.

There is a fine passage in "Captain Craig" where the talkative captain asks: "Is it better to be blinded by the lights, / Or by the shadows?" This supposes grandly that we are to be blinded in any case, but Robinson was not blinded by his shadows. Yet he was ill-served by American Romanticism, though not for the reasons Winters offers. It demands the exuberance

of a Whitman in his fury of poetic incarnation, lest the temptation to join
Ananke come too soon and too urgently to be resisted. Robinson was nearly
a great poet, and would have prospered more if he had been chosen by a
less drastic tradition.

YVOR WINTERS

A Cool Master

Near the middle of the last century, Ralph Waldo Emerson, a sentimental philosopher with a genius for a sudden twisted hardness of words, wrote lines like:

> Daughters of Time, the hypocritic days,
> Muffled and dumb like barefoot dervishes,
> And marching single in an endless file,
> Bring diadems and fagots in their hands.

And it was with Emerson that American poetry may be said to have begun. He was slight enough, but at his best a master, and above all a master of sound. And he began a tradition that still exists.

He was followed shortly by Emily Dickinson, a master of a certain dowdy but undeniably effective mannerism, a spinster who may have written her poems to keep time with her broom. A terrible woman, who annihilated God as if He were her neighbor, and her neighbor as if he were God—all with a leaf or a sunbeam that chanced to fall within her sight as she looked out the window or the door during a pause in her sweeping:

> And we, we placed the hair,
> And drew the head erect;
> And then an awful leisure was,
> Our faith to regulate.

From *Yvor Winters: Uncollected Essays and Reviews.* © 1973 by Janet Lewis Winters. The Swallow Press, 1973.

The woman at her most terrible had the majesty of an erect corpse, a prophet of unspeakable doom; and she spoke through sealed lips. She was greater than Emerson, was one of the greatest poets of our language, but was more or less in the tradition that Emerson began. She and Emerson were probably the only poets of any permanently great importance who occurred in this country during their period.

The tradition of New England hardness has been carried on by Mr. Robinson, in many ways may be said to have reached its pinnacle in Mr. Robinson. This poet, with a wider culture than his predecessors, has linked a suavity of manner to an even greater desperation than that of Dickinson's "The Last Night"—his hardness has become a polished stoniness of vision, of mind.

This man has the culture to know that to those to whom philosophy is comprehensible it is not a matter of the first importance; and he knows that these people are not greatly impressed by a ballyhoo statement of the principles of social or spiritual salvation. A few times he has given his opinion, but quietly and intelligently, and has then passed on to other things. A man's philosophical belief or attitude is certain to be an important part of his milieu, and as a part of his milieu may give rise to perceptions, images. His philosophy becomes a part of his life as does the country in which he was born, and will tinge his vision of the country in which he was born as that country may affect his philosophy. So long as he gives us his own perceptions as they arise in this milieu, he remains an artist. When he becomes more interested in the possible effects of his beliefs upon others, and expounds or persuades, he begins to deal with generalities, concepts (see Croce), and becomes a philosopher, or more than likely a preacher, a mere peddler. This was the fallacy of Whitman and many of the English Victorians, and this is what invalidates nearly all of Whitman's work. Such men forget that it is only the particular, the perception, that is perpetually startling. The generality, or concept, can be pigeonholed, absorbed, and forgotten. And a ballyhoo statement of a concept is seldom a concise one—it is neither fish nor flesh. That is why Whitman is doomed to an eventual dull vacuum that the intricately delicate mind of Plato will never know.

Much praise has fallen to Mr. Robinson because he deals with people, "humanity"; and this is a fallacy of inaccurate brains. Humanity is simply Mr. Robinson's physical milieu; the thing, the compound of the things, he sees. It is not the material that makes a poem great, but the perception and organization of that material. A pigeon's wing may make as great an image as a man's tragedy, and in the poetry of Mr. Wallace Stevens has done so. Mr. Robinson's greatness lies not in the people of whom he has written, but in the perfect balance, the infallible precision, with which he has stated their cases.

Mr. Robinson's work may be classified roughly in two groups—his blank verse, and his more closely rhymed poems, including the sonnets. Of his blank verse, the "Octaves" in *The Children of the Night* fall curiously into a group by themselves, and will be considered elsewhere in this review. The other poems in blank verse may be called sketches—some of people the poet may have known, some of historical figures, some of legendary— and they have all the evanescence, brittleness, of sketches. However, there are passages in many of these poems that anticipate Robert Frost, who in at least one poem, "An Old Man's Winter Night," has used this method with greater effect than its innovator, and has created a great poem. Mr. Frost, of course, leaves more of the bark on his rhythms, achieves a sort of implied colloquialism which has already been too much discussed. But with Frost in mind, consider this passage from "Isaac and Archibald":

> A journey that I made one afternoon
> With Isaac to find out what Archibald
> Was doing with his oats. It was high time
> Those oats were cut, said Isaac; and he feared
> That Archibald—well, he could never feel
> Quite sure of Archibald. Accordingly
> The good old man invited me—that is,
> Permitted me—to go along with him;
> And I, with a small boy's adhesiveness
> To competent old age, got up and went.

The similarity to Frost is marked, as is also the pleasing but not profound quality of the verse. It has a distinction, however, that many contemporaries—French as well as English and American—could acquire to good advantage.

"Ben Jonson Entertains a Man from Stratford," a much praised poem, seems largely garrulous, occasionally brilliant, and always brittle; and one can go on making very similar comments on the other poems in this form, until one comes to those alternately praised and lamented poems, *Merlin* and *Lancelot*. Remembering Tennyson, one's first inclination is to name these poems great, and certainly they are not inconsiderable. But there are long passages of purely literary frittering, and passages that, while they may possess a certain clean distinction of manner, are dry and unremunerative enough. But there are passages in these poems which are finer than any

other blank verse Mr. Robinson has written—dark, massive lines that rise
out of the poem and leave one bitter and empty:

> On Dagonet the silent hand of Merlin
> Weighed now as living iron that held him down
> With a primeval power. Doubt, wonderment,
> Impatience, and a self-accusing sorrow
> Born of an ancient love, possessed and held him
> Until his love was more than he could name,
> And he was Merlin's fool, not Arthur's now:
> "Say what you will, I say that I'm the fool
> Of Merlin, King of Nowhere; which is Here.
> With you for king and me for court, what else
> Have we to sigh for but a place to sleep?"

But passing on from this less important side of Mr. Robinson's work
to his rhymed poems, one finds at least a large number of perfectly executed
poems of a sensitive and feline approach. What effect rhyme, or the intention of rhyme, has upon an artist's product, is a difficult thing to estimate.
The question verges almost upon the metaphysical. The artist, creating,
lives at a point of intensity, and whether the material is consciously digested
before that point is reached, and is simply organized and set down at the
time of creation; or whether the point of intensity is first reached and the
material then drawn out of the subconscious, doubtless depends a good deal
on the individual poet, perhaps on the individual poem. The latter method
presupposes a great deal of previous absorption of sense impressions, and
is probably the more valid, or at least the more generally effective, method.
For the rhythm and the "matter," as they come into being simultaneously
and interdependent, will be perfectly fused and without loose ends. The
man who comes to a form with a definitely outlined matter, will, more than
likely, have to cram or fill before he has finished, and the result is broken.
The second method does not, of course, presuppose rhyme; but it seems
that rhyme, as an obstacle, will force the issue.

The best of Mr. Robinson's poems appear to have come into being very
much in this second fashion. He has spun his images out of a world of sense
and thought that have been a part of him so long that he seems to have
forgot their beginning—has spun these images out as the movement of his
lines, the recurrence of his rhymes, have demanded them. A basic philosophy and emotional viewpoint have provided the necessary unity.

This method inevitably focuses the artist's mind upon the object of the
instant, makes it one with that object, and eliminates practically all individ-

ual "personality" or self-consciousness. The so-called personal touch is reduced to a minimum of technical habit that is bound to accrue in time to
any poet who studies his medium with an eye to his individual needs. The
man of some intelligence who cannot, or can seldom, achieve this condition
of fusion with his object, is driven back to his ingenuity; and this man, if he
have sufficient intelligence or ingenuity, becomes one of the "vigorous per-
sonalities" of poetry; and he misses poetry exactly in so far as his personality is vigorous. Browning, on two or three occasions one of the greatest
of all poets, is, for the most part, simply the greatest of ingenious versifiers.
He was so curious of the quirks with which he could approach an object,
that he forgot the object in admiring, and expecting admiration for, himself.
And it is for this reason that Mr. Robinson, working in more or less the
same field as Browning, is the superior of Browning at almost every turn.

And it is for this reason also that Mr. Robinson's "Ben Jonson" is a
failure. For the poet, while in no wise concerned with his own personality,
is so intent upon the personality of Jonson, his speaker, that, for the sake
of Jonson's vigor, he becomes talkative and eager of identifying mannerism;
and the result is, that Shakespeare, about whom the poem is written, comes
to the surface only here and there, and any actual image almost never.

The following stanza is an example of Mr. Robinson's work at its best:

> And like a giant harp that hums
> On always, and is always blending
> The coming of what never comes
> With what has past and had an ending,
> The city trembles, throbs, and pounds
> Outside, and through a thousand sounds
> The small intolerable drums
> Of Times are like slow drops descending.

And there is the compact, intensely contemplated statement of "Eros Turannos," a poem that is, in forty-eight lines, as complete as a Lawrence novel.
And the nimble trickery of "Miniver Cheevy," as finished a piece of bur-
lesque as one can find in English. A few of us have feared, in the last few
years, that Mr. Robinson was deteriorating; but going through this book
one is reassured. If there is nothing in *The Three Taverns* to equal "Eros
Turannos," there are at least two or three poems as great as any save that
one Mr. Robinson has written; and there is nothing in these last poems to
preclude the possibility of another "Eros Turannos."

Mr. Robinson, as probably the highest point in his tradition, has been
followed by Frost, a more specialized, and generally softer artist. And there

is Gould, who, if he belongs to the tradition at all, is a mere breaking-up of the tradition, a fusion with Whitman. But in considering the work of a man of so varied a genius as Mr. Robinson, it is interesting, if not over-important, to observe the modes of expression that he has anticipated if not actually influenced; even where he has not chosen, or has not been able to develop, these modes.

The resemblance in matter and manner, save for Mr. Robinson's greater suavity, of certain poems, especially the sonnets, in *The Children of the Night,* to the epitaphs in *The Spoon River Anthology,* has been noted by other writers; and I believe it has been said that Mr. Masters was ignorant of the existence of these poems until after the *Anthology* was written. There is little to be said about such a poem as Mr. Robinson's "Luke Havergal":

> No, there is not a dawn in eastern skies
> To rift the fiery night that's in your eyes;
> But there, where western glooms are gathering,
> The dark will end the dark, if anything:
> God slays Himself with every leaf that flies,
> And hell is more than half of paradise.
> No, there is not a dawn in eastern skies—
> In eastern skies.
>
> Out of a grave I come to tell you this,
> Out of a grave I come to quench the kiss
> That flames upon your forehead with a glow
> That blinds you to the way that you must go.

And Mr. Masters's satire has been forestalled and outdone in these early sonnets.

But a more curious and interesting resemblance to a later poet is found in the "Octaves" in the same volume:

> To me the groaning of world-worshippers
> Rings like a lonely music played in hell
> By one with art enough to cleave the walls
> Of heaven with his cadence, but without
> The wisdom or the will to comprehend
> The strangeness of his own perversity,
> And all without the courage to deny
> The profit and the pride of his defeat.

If the actual thought of this passage is not that of Wallace Stevens, nevertheless the quality of the thought, the manner of thinking, as well as the style, quite definitely is. To what extent Mr. Robinson may have influenced this greatest of living and of American poets, one cannot say, but in at least three of the "Octaves," one phase of Mr. Stevens's later work—that of "Le Monocle de Mon Oncle" and other recent and shorter poems—is certainly foreshadowed. Mr. Robinson's sound is inevitably the less rich, the less masterly.

In another of the "Octaves" there are a few lines that suggest the earlier poems of Mr. T. S. Eliot, but the resemblance is fleeting and apparently accidental.

If the tradition of New England seems to be reaching an end in the work of Mr. Frost, Mr. Robinson has at least helped greatly in the founding of a tradition of culture and clean workmanship that such poets as Messrs. Stevens, Eliot, and Pound, as H. D. and Marianne Moore, are carrying on. Mr. Robinson was, when he began, as much a pioneer as Mr. Pound or Mr. Yeats, and he has certainly achieved as great poetry. While the tradition begun, more or less, by Whitman has deteriorated, in the later work of Mr. Carl Sandburg, into a sort of plasmodial delirium; and while the school of mellifluous and almost ominous stage-trappings, as exemplified by Poe, has melted into a sort of post-Celtic twilight, and has nearly vanished in the work of Mr. Aiken; the work of these writers and a few others stands out clear and hard in the half-light of our culture. I cannot forget that they exist, even in the face of the desert.

ROY HARVEY PEARCE

The Old Poetry and the New: Robinson

The master-songs are ended?
—ROBINSON, "Walt Whitman"

At the beginning of this century, American poetry had relapsed into a half-life. In the 1880s and after, as the promise of American life appeared uncertain and confused, so did the promise of American poetry. The popular audience had become so diffused as to lose its ascertainable identity, and the elite audience for the most part had become uncomfortable with elite poetry precisely because it was elite. The American poet could no longer afford to figure himself as no more (and no less) than an unreconstructed Adam who had only to behold his world in order to bring it alive and make it worthy of the beholding. His impulse had been essentially lyrical, even when it had achieved epic expression; and it had been grounded in his assurance that he might write verses which would be resonant with his sense of wholeness and radical freedom, at once noble and terrible, which American life promised. He was free, as though for the first time in history, to confront the facts of life as they really were; such freedom followed from an assurance that in the United States the force and fullness of existence, in all its good and evil, was available to the poet as it was to no other man. He had taken upon himself the obligation to demonstrate that life in the United States, if properly conceived and expressed, could not run counter to his instinctive hopes for it—which were those of man at his moments of profoundest insight into his freedom to make his way in the world. But now American culture, its destiny no longer clearly and simply manifest, was being torn asunder by its own increasingly depersonalized, mechanized,

From *The Continuity of American Poetry.* © 1961 by Princeton University Press.

bureaucratized power to move men and mountains. The poet could only name what he witnessed, not transform it. He was in the position of the first Adam, cast out of his new world. But he had no Raphael to give him a vision of the ultimate rightness of his fall from his natural state.

There were enough such witnesses, however—poets only in so far as the fiction they wrote is poetry. Naturalistic and realistic novelists, probers in depth of the structure of American culture and of the men and women whose lives it shaped, the major writers of the Gilded Age and after—novelists almost all of them—came again and again to study the failure of the very impulse which had made of American poets an identifiable group doing an identifiable thing. The protagonists of such novels—Huck Finn, Lambert Strether, Silas Lapham, Sister Carrie (to name some of the greatest among them)—are characteristically persons whose capacity to be, or to want to be, themselves is so great as to be charismatic. Yet when they succeed, pathetically or tragically, it is at the expense of their own greatness. They cannot finally commit themselves to American life, for it will furnish them neither the means nor the substance to sustain themselves as authentic, whole persons. They flee American civilization, having been there before; or they transcend it; or they ride the crest of one of its waves, watching those below them who drown. If the continuity of American poetry seems to have been broken for a time, yet the continuity of the spirit it celebrated carried on. For if the poet could no longer see his way clear to be his own hero, at least he was, under personae other than his own, the hero of a good many novels—novels in which his heroism was measured by his ability to make something of himself, all the while refusing to yield to that world which would render him unable to make anything out of anything.

In 1885, in his *Poets of America,* Edmund Stedman, then Cham of American critics, declared that one great age in American poetry was over and as yet no other great age was coming anew. This was an "interregnum," he said. He admired Whitman, but was troubled by his pointless experiments in form; Emerson, but was puzzled by his love for "woodnotes wild"; Poe, but condemned his elevating "taste" over "justice." He was convinced beyond doubt, however, of the greatness of the Fireside Poets. He still held to their hope for the great audience. But he could see only disaster in the tendency of poets who were his contemporaries to cut themselves off from their readers: "If, then, the people care little for current poetry, is it not because that poetry cares little for the people and fails to assume its vantage-ground? Busying itself with intricacies of form and sound and imagery, it scarcely deigns to reach the general heart." The authentic popular poetry of an age immediately past, whose power and authority he blindly overestimates, caused in Stedman a nostalgia so pervasive as to make him hope that the achievements of the age were not only of the highest sort but that they might well point the way to something even higher. Yet he was perceptive enough to know that whatever kind of poetry might come, it would not be the sort to which he was accustomed.

He sensed that the conditions of modern life had brought with them a "new Americanism" and that there was needed for poetry, as for all the literary arts, an adequately "realistic method": "[We] crave the sensations of mature and cosmopolitan experience, and are bent upon what we are told is the proper study of mankind. The rise of our novelists was the answer to this craving; they depict *Life* as it is, though rarely as yet in its intenser phases." How treat of life in its intenser phases? This was something that Stedman's contemporaries, so eager (as he said) to burst into song, somehow had not learned, or had forgotten. Yet in an age whose fiction was given over to the wondrous extremes of "veritism" and the Jamesian center of consciousness, it seemed inevitable, as a *Dial* critic said in 1910, that the interregnum would begin to end with nothing less than a "new belief in poetry."

Here is a characteristic list [by Richard Crowder] of some poets prominent in the latter part of the nineteenth century and the earlier part of the twentieth: "Riley and Field; the Negro Paul Laurence Dunbar; the lady poets Edith Matilda Thomas, Louise Chandler Moulton, Elizabeth Stoddard, Louise Imogen Guiney, and Lizette Woodworth Reese; the perfectionists Aldrich, Gilder, Bunner, and Sherman; Ambrose Bierce, Emily Dickinson, Richard Hovey, Stephen Crane, Father Tabb, Henry Van Dyke, Madison Cawein, Lloyd Mifflin, and George Santayana." We might add two more names—Moody and Stickney. Still, this is a depressing list, especially if we remember that Emily Dickinson as yet had no reputation and few readers and that Crane and Santayana did not yet count for much as poets—nor, I think, should they now. On the whole, these poets were *fin-de-siècle* romantics, even when they tried (as did Moody and Stickney) to work toward a "classical" revival. Their poems are, in the bad sense, exercises in rhetoric, too-delicate evocations of the trivial or too-robust summonings-up of the "sublime." They feel like poets but do not write like them—now over-excited, now playing it too safe, utterly at a loss to deal with live situations in live language; for all their sense of dedication, more interested in being creative than in creating.

The list is useful, however, not only as a *vade mecum,* but for the fact that it occurs in a recent essay on Edwin Arlington Robinson. Robinson's achievement is crucial in this account of the seeming break in the continuity of American poetry. For Robinson at his best transformed the characteristically egocentric nineteenth-century poem into a vehicle to express the exhaustion and failure of its primary impulse. At his worst, by sheer doggedness he tried to move beyond exhaustion, in the hope of finding a new source of strength whereby that impulse might be renewed. He showed, in the first case, that the egocentric poem, if it were to be made a viable mode for twentieth-century poets, had to be reconceived in the light of the nature of twentieth-century American culture—increasingly depersonalized, mechanized, bureaucratized—and the sort of antipoetics its peculiar language manifested. He showed, in the second case, that there needed to be yet another poetic mode, if the twentieth-century writer were somehow to comprehend what his commitment to an infinitude of songs of himself might cost him. He showed the need, that is to say, for what I shall presently have occasion to call the *mythic* poem, and indeed in his later years tried to write it.

Robinson, in short, invented his own variations on the nineteenth-century basic style and made it into an instrument for poetic fictions in which protagonists and circumstances so interpenetrate as to result in that marvelous complex of self-discovery and self-deceit which characterize the sort of understanding available to his modern men. Significantly, his poems at their best are anecdotal, tending toward the tale and thus toward the novelistic. Mediating between the realism of the best fiction of his time and the analytic and evocative power of poetry in the egocentric mode, the Adamic mode, Robinson's best poems expound life in its "intenser phases." The intensity is great to the degree that the phases, the slices of life, are narrow and constrained, quickly exhausted of their potentiality for freedom and joy.

Robinson recognized the major voice in American poetry before his own time, a voice now falsely echoed by many, even as he who owned it was being virtually deified by his followers. The voice was Walt Whitman's; and Robinson acknowledged its power in a poem apparently written soon after Whitman's death:

> The master-songs are ended, and the man
> That sang them is a name. And so is God
> A name; and so is love, and life, and death,
> And everything. But we, who are too blind
> To read what we have written, or what faith
> Has written for us, do not understand:
> We only blink, and wonder.

Last night it was the song that was the man,
But now it is the man that is the song.
We do not hear him very much to-day:
His piercing and eternal cadence rings
Too pure for us—too powerfully pure,
Too lovingly triumphant, and too large;
But there are some that hear him, and they know
That he shall sing to-morrow for all men,
And that all time shall listen.

The master-songs are ended? Rather say
No songs are ended that are ever sung,
And that no names are dead names. When we write
Men's letters on proud marble or on sand,
We write them there forever.

("Walt Whitman")

Robinson here states his vocation and at the same time tries to comprehend its immediate history. A great age in American poetry is over; what once were songs have become mere concatenations of words; Whitman's power, purity, and largeness are too much for the present age, as is his conception of the expressive force of language. Still, poetry, not Whitman's but Robinson's, is yet possible, as it must always be possible.

Robinson wanted to define exactly the area of possibility. The area was perforce narrower than that which Whitman could master; for it is one filled with such figures as find no place in Whitman's poetry—men and women whose egocentrism persists, but as a means of mere survival, not of making and doing, least of all of communicating or of bringing others alive. Above all, these are the dwellers in Tilbury Town. Richard Cory, Charles Carville, Miniver Cheevy, Luke Havergal, Aunt Imogen, Briony (of "Fragment"), Cliff Klingenhagen—these and others like them people that small world of which Robinson could make himself so completely the master. It is a village world, to be sure, but a village world whose sense of community has been destroyed. Most of its inhabitants are failures: sometimes resigned to their failure, sometimes unresignedly crushed by it. They have no means of declaring directly their sense of themselves; if such a sense exists, we are given to know it only inferentially, as, putting himself in the position of the inevitable outsider, Robinson can make us know it. They are in and of themselves not expressive; they have lost the power, if they have had it, of direct communication. The kind of communication which is transformative creation—the gift which the major poets of the American Renaissance were so sure was innate in all men—this is completely beyond them, does not even exist as a memory. Even the relative successes like Flammonde cannot communicate. Still, whatever their degree of failure or success, they are as persons meaningful to us. For they signify something important in the nature of the modern psyche—even if it is only as they are made to recall, in their inability to communicate directly, a condition and a time when such a thing as self-reliance (in any of its various forms) was a radical possibility for all men. In them, Robinson pushes to an outer limit a sense of the exhaustion, perhaps the bankruptcy, of the simple, separate person. Tilbury Town is the underworld of Walden and Paumanok.

Some of them live on by means of their profound illusions about themselves and their world. Some of them are beyond having such illusions. Often they are made out to be illusory to both their fellow townspeople and to the poet. For the Robinson who writes about them, understanding them is in the end making guesses about them, wondering about them. Indeed, it is a sense of puzzled wonderment which enables Robinson to treat of them at all:

> How much it was of him we met
> We cannot ever know; nor yet
> Shall all he gave us quite atone
> For what was his, and his alone;
> Nor need we now, since he knew best,
> Nourish an ethical unrest:
> Rarely at once will nature give
> The power to be Flammonde and live.
>
> ("Flammonde")

> There are the pillars, and all gone gray.
> Briony's hair went white. You may see
> Where the garden was if you come this way.
> That sun-dial scared him, he said to me;
> "Sooner or later they strike," said he,
> And he never got that from the books he read.
> Others are flourishing, worse than he,
> But he knew too much for the life he led.
>
> ("Fragment")

Flammonde and Briony, for Robinson, have this in common: that whatever they are, whatever they know, however they have succeeded and failed, the poet can only report his discovery that something unanalyzably vital is involved, and then wonder at it. Like a novelist, he wonders at, and so celebrates, the simple perdurability of life lived through; its meaning for man lies in the fact that it can be endured. It is enough to confront life as a fact—or would have been, had Robinson eventually found his proper (as I think) métier as novelist. So it is that in the end he understands those who are still living no better than those who are dead—Amaryllis, Hector Kane, the Dead Lady, the wife of the owner of The Mill, for example. He best understands the living dead—Mr. Flood, old Isaac and Archibald, and the rest; for their state is the most direct and powerful metaphor for the spirit which is the *communitas* of Tilbury Town. The ending of "Mr. Flood's Party" calls up that sense of loneliness and deprivation which informs so many of Robinson's poems:

> The weary throat gave out,
> The last word wavered, and the song was done.
> He raised again the jug regretfully
> And shook his head, and was again alone.
> There was not much that was ahead of him,
> And there was nothing in the town below—
> Where strangers would have shut the many doors
> That many friends had opened long ago.

Robinson has no illusions about the fate of this man—not even enough to comment, in the manner of one of Melville's narrators, "Ah Mr. Flood! Ah humanity!" Nor has Mr. Flood, nor any of the others, the power to say even "I prefer not to."

How, then, communicate not only about but for those who themselves cannot? This was Robinson's great problem; and his achievement as a poet lies in the fact that he so often solves it, and solving it, marks the outermost limit of even a vaguely (posthumously, as it were) Adamic poem. Above all, here Robinson writes as an outsider; but then, in this world no one is on the inside. Thus his poems are mainly in the third person; when they are in the first, they are still somehow in the third, consisting of the speeches of actors who are quite self-conscious as regards the masks they are assuming. Moreover, the poems are not really expressive of the psyches of their protagonists; rather they are expressive of the poet's, and putatively the reader's, mode of understanding them. (It is worth observing parenthetically that the failure of such a poet as Robinson's contemporary, Edgar Lee Masters, lies in his insistence on trying to make his poems directly expressive of the aspirations of those who tell us their stories. Yet they too are defeated;

and Masters, unable to understand the nature of their defeat, renders them
only as they are repetitiously pathetic.) Robinson's poems are dramatic
rather than lyrical; they have, at their best, a certain conclusive, clean-cut
objectivity, lacking even in Emerson's and Whitman's poems of the natural
scene. For Emerson and Whitman were constantly engaged in transforming
the natural scene, invoking it. Robinson will merely see it, and the people
in it, merely call it to mind, evoke it. So Robinson moves from the expressive freedom of the line composed by his forebears to a line characterized
by hard objectivity and tense restriction. He loads his lines with almost
prosaic locutions; he is compressed rather than expansive; he seeks control
rather than release. The poem is all *there,* even when it frames a vacuous
situation, and does not depend for its power upon a consonance with the
largest ranges of its reader's experience. It is, in a word, an end in itself, not
a beginning toward something else. Robinson controls meters so as to
achieve analytic power, as he controls rhyme too. With such control—and
often with explicit statement—he tells us that *he* is there, as an observer;
and he thus makes of us observers too, outsiders with him. He uses such
traditional forms, the sonnet in particular, as will let him get a self-
consciously formalized hold on his material. He is a self-consciously "literary" poet, one who goes to other poets quite deliberately to learn how to
see his world and compose it. Yet he puts what he learns to his own needs—
which are to be an American poet, writing in an American tradition, for an
American community whom that tradition has failed. The achievement of
his technique is one of discovering how to record, with a frigid passion, the
limitations of the expressivism cultivated by the major American poets before him. His technique is, of course, one with his meaning.

This is the great Robinson. Here, for example, is "Eros Turannos," a
depiction of the mind and fate of one who dwells in Tilbury Town:

> She fears him, and will always ask
>   What fated her to choose him;
> She meets in his engaging mask
>   All reasons to refuse him;
> But what she meets and what she fears
> Are less than are the downward years,
> Drawn slowly to the foamless weirs
>   Of age, were she to lose him.
>
> Between a blurred sagacity
>   That once had power to sound him,

And Love, that will not let him be
   The Judas that she found him,
Her pride assuages her almost,
As if it were alone the cost.—
He sees that he will not be lost,
   And waits and looks around him.

A sense of ocean and old trees
   Envelopes and allures him;
Tradition, touching all he sees,
   Beguiles and reassures him;
And all her doubts of what he says
Are dimmed with what she knows of days—
Till even prejudice delays
   And fades, and she secures him.

The falling leaf inaugurates
   The reign of her confusion;
The pounding wave reverberates
   The dirge of her illusion;
And home, where passion lived and died,
Becomes a place where she can hide,
While all the town and harbor side
   Vibrate with her seclusion.

We tell you, tapping on our brows,
   The story as it should be,—
As if the story of a house
   Were told, or ever could be;
We'll have no kindly veil between
Her visions and those we have seen,—
As if we guessed what hers have been,
   Or what they are or would be.

Meanwhile we do no harm; for they
   That with a god have striven,
Not hearing much of what we say,
   Take what the god has given;
Though like waves breaking it may be,
Or like a changed familiar tree,

Or like a stairway to the sea
Where down the blind are driven.

Again, the protagonist is a failure; again, it is the fact of her isolation that interests the poet. He goes so far in the fifth stanza as to confess that his account of her, the account of a community of outsiders, is one raised to the level of art and therefore not necessarily true to the facts of her life—"The story as it should be." The poet as outsider can only make an object-lesson of her, the knowledge of which is an end in itself. She is, in effect, the excuse for the poem, not its subject. She will not (or cannot) "express" her sense of her fate; an outsider perforce cannot do so; he can, however, analyze it as it might strike the community, and put it in the perspective of his understanding of the general fate of people such as she.

The first four lines quite bluntly present her situation; the rest of the first stanza, introducing the weirs-sea image, goes more deeply, as it discovers something symbolic in her fate—though the image, nominally a symbol, is so restricted and controlled as to operate as a simile. The poem, elaborating that symbol, or simile, is in the end not a detailed and evocative exploration of her soul, but rather a kind of monument to it. Robinson is at his best at such monumental poetry; he shows what the graveyard (or gravestone) poem really can be. He assumes for most of his protagonists an inevitable, walled-off privacy; sensing the failure of that "individualism" traditionally associated with New England towns, he would again and again show that it is no longer possible to summon up a feeling of genuine community and solidarity on the basis of such individualism. So he seeks to memorialize it, to put on record the failure of Americans (or some Americans) to be persons. What he seeks to do demands an ability to discover such similitudes as are in "Eros Turannos," to make out his subjects as they are, above all, objects—waiting for public inspection, analysis, and understanding.

There is thus the tendency of many of the packed lines of "Eros Turannos" to function almost as proverbs and epigrams; we learn lessons. There is the carry-through to the end of the weirs-sea figure introduced in the third stanza. We are not allowed to forget that we are listening to a master-rhetorician. In the fourth stanza, we are told, not that the "falling leaf" is somehow sympathetically expressive of her "confusion," but that it simply "inaugurates" it—i.e., at once gives and marks a beginning. Directly after this, we are told that the "pounding wave reverberates / the dirge of her illusion"—where again the expressive significance is minimized and the memorializing significance, the similitude, made most important. Too, the waves' reverberation is one with the town's vibration, but there is no hint of any kind of transnatural "correspondence" here, just a sense of a rhetorical device powerfully used to direct our attention as the poet-observer wills. So it goes: the figurative language, the rhymes (especially the feminine rhymes, which have the effect of easing the epigrammatic bite, making the lines subside rather than end sharply), and the stanzaic structure—each has this powerfully memorializing effect. At the end, the public meaning of a closed-off, private life is put in such a way that it can be openly confronted, but by the reader, not the protagonist. We do no harm to her real self to make her a vehicle for an understanding of man's fate, the poet assures us. For us, she may be said to have striven with a god, grateful for what she might get from him. And then, magnificently, yet rather marmoreally, the weirs-sea and the tree figure are made to resolve the whole.

With the Robinson of "Eros Turannos," much as we would like to be more, we can only be witnesses. With his forebears we could have been celebrants. But now we write poems, and read them, in order to make bearable our understanding that the truth is that, if we are heroic, we can be true only to ourselves, not to one another. The Adamic glow is no longer strong enough to light up the American community; and yet it is, for this Robinson, all we have. Our only certitude lies in our incertitude.

Robinson was terribly restive under the burden of such an incertitude. He felt deeply that something had been lost and wanted as deeply to find it again. The poems of the sort which I have been discussing—in which for the most part he quite simply confronts and portrays that loss, not trying to account for it—are mainly from his early and middle period, written before 1920. In many of them there is evidence of his restiveness. It takes the form most often of the kind of image he associates with those in whom some of his lonely, isolated failures believe, or try to believe. They are not only mysterious; they seem to generate a supernatural light. The people of the town have "each a darkening hill to climb," but beyond the darkness they see Flammonde (whose name itself indicates his light-giving properties). The mother who in "The Gift of God" idolizes her quite unremarkable son, is made to think of him repeatedly (and Bunyan is echoed here, of course) as a "shining one." "Old King Cole" attracts men as "He beamed as with an inward light." (That this is an ironically used Quakerism does not lessen its significance.) We are told of the protagonist of "Old Trails" that "His memories are like lamps, and they go out; / Or if they burn, they flicker and are dim. / A light of other gleams he has to-day." The abundance of statements of this kind indicate some sort of compulsive habit of mind; they show how natural it was for Robinson to want to proceed beyond his great achievement in the objectified, limited and limiting poem. In the end he was desperate, wanting to abolish the aesthetic distance (achieved in such ways as are manifest in "Eros Turannos") which separated him from the objects of his poems. He had within him a good deal of that old Adamic longing to subjectify his objects, to see more clearly what their inner light revealed, to discover such light in himself and then to report the discovery to the world at large.

He wanted in the end to be as much a philosophical as a dramatic poet. Philosophical poetry was to be his means of establishing the sense of *communitas*—of ego-transcending human relations—which dramatic poetry requires. At this he failed just about completely. The great, the pathetic, example is "The Man against the Sky." It is a confused and confusing poem, because Robinson cannot contrive the kind of subjective analysis he wants to make and yet hold to an adequate memorializing perspective on his protagonists. Indeed, they are hardly protagonists; they are given no life of their own; their problems are talked about, not projected directly into language; they are in no specific and clearly meaningful way caught up in the life of their milieu. They are symbols of a most inferior sort—neither in themselves expressive enough to evoke a sense of their inner life as men, nor given enough objectivity to have an outward station, and thus furnish an apt similitude. The trouble is that they are separated from the light and made to move toward it, while the poet wonders what their moving means; whereas in the earlier poems this mysterious light was constitutive of the nature of the men themselves, and it was in effect not light per se but light-bearing men to whom the poet was attracted. The poet himself is too much involved in "The Man against the Sky"; he allegorizes aspects of himself. Yet he has no such solid foundation, no such cultural certitude, no such assurance of a community of believers, as will allow him to construct proper allegory. In proper allegory we can assent to the actions of the protagonists because the sum total of those actions is a manifestation of an authoritative system of belief, aspects of which we expect their actions to body forth. But Robinson, in "The Man against the Sky," as elsewhere, is determined to establish the system of belief even as he studies the actions of those to whose lives it gives meaning.

Of the man who moves against sky, toward the light, Robinson says after a series of lengthy sections dealing with his various possible motivations:

> Whatever drove or lured or guided him,—
> A vision answering a faith unshaken,

An easy trust assumed of easy trials,
A sick negation born of weak denials,
A crazed abhorrence of an old condition,
A blind attendance on a brief ambition,—
Whatever stayed him or derided him,
His way was even as ours;
And we, with all our wounds and all our powers,
Must each await alone at his own height
Another darkness or another light.

Each of these alternatives represents a mode of existence; but it is here not men who exist, but rather vague projections of vaguely imagined possibilities. Robinson, who really had little power of empathy, is honest enough, in the last four lines quoted, virtually to withdraw his claim that these are in any way valid or inclusive types; for we "Must each await alone." If, as one argues with Robinson ex post facto, we must wait alone, how can we construct any kind of typology of the sort the poem aims at? For every man, as the earlier poems demonstrate, is himself and no one else. His meaning as man lies precisely in his being no one but himself, and must be memorialized as such.

Whereas Whitman was able, through the exercise of his powerful egocentrism, to deal with all simple, separate persons and things as ultimately constituting a single, vibrant community, Robinson, in seeking a sense of community, perforce erases all simplicity and separateness and constructs a community of only himself. For all its antipoetics, Whitman's world was still simply enough constituted (or the memory of such simplicity was fresh enough in his mind) to allow, even to encourage, him to exercise his egocentrism thus. Robinson had neither a world like Whitman's nor the sort of sensibility whose most powerful operations such a world would encourage. Yet he could in the end not quite free himself of his specifically Whitmanian, Adamic longings. ("The master-songs are ended?" he had written, the question mark looming larger and larger as time passed.) He too yearned after that transcendental principle which, however paradoxically, would authorize the Adamic way. Yet everything about him belied such a principle. So he tried to conjure it into existence. Thus "The Man against the Sky" fails to the degree that Robinson's technique and the imagination which informs it fail. They will let him study other men, but only from the outside. They are not adequate to the task of delineating any inwardness except that of the poet who knows, even if he forgets the fact, only his own.

So that, toward the end of "The Man against the Sky" the poet can only chant his ode to himself; even here his writing is not as strong as it is in the shorter poems, because he strives to express that which his own faith—and the technique it called forth—says is inexpressible:

> Where was he going, this man against the sky?
> You know not, nor do I.
> But this we know, if we know anything:
> That we may laugh and fight and sing
> And of our transcience here make offering
> To an orient Word that will not be erased,
> Or, save in incommunicable gleams,
> Too permanent for dreams,
> Be found or known.

This is transcendentalism of a sort, to be sure—but transcendentalism without the crucial doctrine of Emerson's Nature and thus without Emerson's (and Whitman's) sense of the contingency and oneness of all things. There is lacking a principle of control whereby one thing the poet says follows necessarily from what precedes it. Control derives from technique, technique from commitment to a theory of action and motivation; the theory must be such as to enable the poet to conceive integrally of the nature of a man and the world which, as he makes it, makes him. Here there is a man, but not a world with which his being is consonant. Failing this, the images are trite and the movement so irregular and discontinuous as to give the passage none of that fluid stability which characterizes Robinson's verse at its best. The poet too often strives to hint at what he has no way of imagining. The poem needs a situation and a movement more certain than those dictated by the poet's compulsion, however genuine, to see the light.

Robinson's great strength lies in the fact that, faced with the divisiveness of the modern world (see his "Cassandra," for example), he would not settle for a merely putative sense of oneness. Yet he longed for that sense. As New England American poet, perhaps he could not throw off his Adamic heritage, even as he saw that it was not enough. After writing poems in which he demonstrated, substantively and formally, that it was not enough, he found his own capacities drained. He looked for more than his talent, his heritage, his sensibility, and his technique would allow him to find, or to see. In his first long poem, "Captain Craig," he allowed his protagonist to speak in the first person, and thereby, it is true, failed to achieve the sharpness of insight and outline of the shorter poems. Yet he put well the sense of one who knew himself to be distinctively post-transcendentalist (and I daresay, post-Adamic):

"I cannot think of anything to-day
That I would rather do than be myself,
Primevally alive, and have the sun
Shine into me; for on a day like this
When chaff-parts of a man's adversities
Are blown by quick spring breezes out of him—
When even a flicker of wind that wakes no more
Than a tuft of grass, or a few young yellow leaves,
Comes like the falling of a prophet's breath
On altar-flames rekindled of crushed embers,—
Then do I feel, now do I feel, within me
No dreariness, no grief, no discontent
No twinge of human envy."

All this is fine; and it recalls the opening of Emerson's "Divinity School Address": "In this refulgent summer, it has been a luxury to draw the breath of life." But Captain Craig is Robinson's ideal protagonist, an Emersonian in extremis, who fails so completely that he is a success at it. He dies saying only "Trombones" (which he wanted for his funeral) as Thoreau had died saying "Indians" (of whom he wanted to treat in a last great book).

The later long poems—*Merlin* (1917), *Lancelot* (1920), *Roman Bartholow* (1923), *Tristram* (1927), *King Jasper* (1935), and the rest—are only to be regretted. There is no one like Captain Craig in any of them; there are no persons in any of them, just aspects of the disintegrated psyche of a disintegrated community, without even strong memories of what it had been. When Robinson wanted to move away from those great memorializing poems of his, when he wanted something more than stoic objectivity, he turned to myth and to full-blown allegory. He was simply not equipped to write mythic or allegorical poems. Yet, however agonizingly, he saw the need for a means to a poetic objectivity so great, a perspective so deep, as to urge him to leave behind—because it was not enough—the egocentric poem of his heritage. He would proceed to another kind, in which men, having given up the hope to express themselves, might learn to be expressed by the forms of their own world and of whatever world might be beyond it. Robinson wanted to be a yea-sayer (as who doesn't?). But he could, at his best, be no more than a nay-sayer. Even so, he could not say No! in thunder. In his most powerful work the Adamic yea of the continuity of American poetry, confronting its failure to transform its world into an image of its heroic yea-saying self, can only admit defeat. But the Adamic impulse still holds and still shows its value. For, yea or nay, it is the impulse

to be honest. This, surely, is what Robinson contributed to American poetry; this is his place in its continuity. Coming out of a time of sentimental-
ists, poetasters, androgynous Adams, and their bluestocking Eves—a barren time for the life of American poetry—he could, at his moments of
greatness, in the midst of his later failures, yet rise to the strength and honesty of his "Wandering Jew" of 1920:

> He may have died so many times
> That all there was of him to see
> Was pride, that kept itself alive
> As too rebellious to be free;
> He may have told, when more than once
> Humility seemed imminent,
> How many a lonely time in vain
> The Second Coming came and went.
>
> Whether he still defies or not
> The failure of an angry task
> That relegates him out of time
> To chaos, I can only ask.
> But as I knew him, so he was;
> And somewhere among men to-day
> Those old, unyielding eyes may flash,
> And flinch—and look the other way.

DENIS DONOGHUE

A Poet of Continuing Relevance

In 1933 Edwin Arlington Robinson was the "most famous of living American poets." Today his good gray name is attached to a handful of short poems that are exhibited in the respectable anthologies. But he is no longer an audible voice in poetry except to those sturdy readers who take time to wonder why the long poems are not as good as they should be, or to a few rigorous and lonely poets who find Robinson, for one reason or another, indispensable. But if one poet is indispensable to another, the reason is likely to be interesting. To come upon Robert Lowell reading Crabbe's tales, for instance, is to witness a strange and exhilarating encounter. And if such authority issues from a poet as relentlessly unfashionable as Robinson, we are almost obliged to attend to it. Our text is the *Collected Poems,* a daunting book of almost fifteen hundred pages.

In offering Robinson as a poet of continuing relevance we shall find it necessary to make some concessions, and it is well to make them sooner rather than later. And it may even be useful to give the largest concession immediately. If we think of T. S. Eliot as perhaps in the highest degree a characteristic poet of this century, then we must concede at once that Robinson either did not know or was indifferent to the movements of feeling that lead to Eliot's revolutionary poems. And we know that such ignorance, such indifference, are hard sins to forgive. We think, for a nearer comparison, of Yeats, almost an exact contemporary, only four years older than Robinson. Genius apart, Yeats clearly ploughs a deeper furrow. We have only to compare Yeats's "Upon a Dying Lady" with Robinson's "For a Dead

From *Connoisseurs of Chaos.* © 1964, 1984 by Denis Donoghue. Columbia University Press, 1984.

Lady" to see that Yeats took far greater risks of sensibility and that he seized the advantage of a much deeper personal and social context in which to work. Robinson's lady dies and proves what the poets have always told us, that time is a vicious reaper, going far beyond the duties of his post. Yeats's lady dies not to make a point or to show herself a tragic heroine. A certain kind of death fittingly concludes a certain kind of life, thereby endorsing both; to embody this is her task. Yeats exposed himself to the contingency of other people and knew that the image of his work would have to fit the squirming facts. Robinson at an early age came to know certain things, and he thought that there was nothing else to know. These things became his property, and we have them in the poems in that capacity. Many of the later poems are attempts to protect his property in an age of subversion and falling prices. The things he knew were, for the most part, the old terms, old categories, and he thought that they would serve every occasion. And perhaps in the long run they will. But Robinson underestimated the pressure they would have to bear. A term like "sincerity" is a case in point. Now, after Gide and Mann and D. H. Lawerence, we may still be ignorant of its meaning, but at least we know that the meaning is elusive. Robinson uses the word as if it were his property, impregnable. In "Captain Craig," for instance, he says:

> Take on yourself
> But your sincerity, and you take on
> Good promise for all-climbing.

Again, Robinson pushed his property very hard. He put great stock in the idea of vision and action, and indeed a major theme is the disproportion between the two, the gap between what one can see and what one can realize in action. But it is not endless in its resource. Robinson keeps nudging us to witness his theme and to acknowledge that it is his very own. In *Merlin*, for instance, Vivian says:

> Like you, I saw too much; and unlike you
> I made no kingdom out of what I saw—

But if this is Vivian it might equally be any one of twenty speakers in Robinson's poems. People in these poems see too much, or else they see it too late. Either way they are frustrate, and like Seneca Sprague they visit some of their frustration upon the reader, who has heard it all from Robinson before. Too much or too late; we are born at a bad time; vision and action do not synchronize. After a while, in Robinson's poems, this note begins to sound like a list of rules for membership in a gloom club. Robert Frost, irritated by one of George Russell's platitudes in the same key, wrote a splendid poem to say that the times are neither wrong nor right. Robinson never confronted this fantastic possibility, though he could have found it easily by consulting Emily Dickinson. In book 9 of *Tristram* Mark walks the battlements, groaning, "Had I known early / All that I knew too late." We hear this again in *Amaranth* and in many other poems. In *King Jasper* it isn't even a matter of vision—everything that happens comes, like Zoë, too late. Robinson's trains are scheduled never to arrive on time; we are all men against the sky. To use the terms of "The Wandering Jew," "the figure and the scene / Were never to be reconciled." Robinson became more and more lugubrious about this in his later poems. Indeed, "Miniver Cheevy" is the only poem in which he treats it lightly, and it is one of his finest poems for that very reason:

> Miniver Cheevy, born too late,
>   Scratched his head and kept on thinking:
> Miniver coughed, and called it fate,
>   And kept on drinking.

Robinson came to lose this note, and it passed to other hands, notably to John Crowe Ransom in "Captain Carpenter." And in his later years Robinson felt that life consisted entirely of ironies great and little, and he became their devoted chronicler. Indeed, this was true to such an extent that when a phrase from a Robinson poem lodges in the mind or comes up unbidden, it is invariably a gray generalization like "the sunlit labyrinth of pain," "time's malicious mercy," "time's offending benefits," "the patient ardor of the unpursued," or "a dry gasp of affable despair." And the fretful note increased, especially after "The Man against the Sky." Robinson's favorite color was gray, while most readers have now been schooled to prefer, if anything in that line, downright black. Hence we feel that poems like *Cavender's House* have everything that a good poem needs except variety, so that even the well-made sounds become dull, like the "sequestered murmuring" of "Captain Craig." (There is a letter of Hopkins to Baillie in 1864 in which he offers terms for a discrimination of styles, and one of these he calls "Parnassian." This is a kind of style that is all too characteristic of its author. And Hopkins says that when a poet palls on us it is because of his Parnassian: we "seem to have found out his secret." Robinson has a great deal of Parnassian in those fifteen hundred pages.)

     If we need a phrase to stand for these concessions, Robinson gives one in "The Glory of the Nightingales" when he speaks of "the embellished rhetoric of regret." This is the signature tune of his work, or much of it, apart from its greatest occasions. In *Amaranth* the stranger says:

> I am one Evensong, a resident
> For life in the wrong world, where I made music,
> And make it still. It is not necessary,
> But habit that has outlived revelation
> May pipe on to the end.

And so, alas, it does. But we are almost finished with concession.

It is usual to say that Robinson's good work is to be found in the short narratives, that the long poems are stuffed with sentimental heroes, tragic ironies, melancholy, and moral earnestness. This is a little unfair. None of the long poems is a complete success, but none except *Amaranth* is a mere failure. There are passages and often entire books in the long poems that are remarkable achievements. But I must be specific. Robinson's successful poems seem to me to be these: from *The Man against the Sky,* "Hillcrest," "Eros Turannos," "The Unforgiven," "Veteran Sirens," "Another Dark Lady," "The Poor Relation," and with some reservations, the title poem itself; from *The Children of the Night,* "Aaron Stark," "Luke Havergal," "Cliff Klingenhagen," "Fleming Helphenstine," "Reuben Bright," "The Altar," "George Crabbe." (I would not include the famous "Richard Cory," which seems to me a contrived piece.) From *Captain Craig* I would select "Isaac and Archibald," which is much better than the title poem, and I would add "The Growth of 'Lorraine.' " The last book of *Merlin* is particularly good, but there are fine passages also in the third and seventh books. From *The Town down the River* I would choose "The Master" and "Miniver Cheevy." *Lancelot* is hardly worth its ninety pages, but the conversation between Lancelot and Guinevere in the last book is memorable. In *The Three Taverns* the indispensable poems are "The Mill," "Souvenir," *Avon's Harvest,* "Mr. Flood's Party." *Tristram* is also essential, and we will return to it. From *Dionysus in Doubt* I prefer "Haunted House," "The Sheaves," "Karma," "Maya," "Mortmain," and "New England." And at this point, with one-fifth of the *Collected Poems* still in front of us, we have had the best of it. The last narratives are all habit, little revelation.

Some of the poems I have named are famous and have been in the common possession for many years. "Eros Turannos," for instance, is a masterpiece, and "The Mill" is equally fine. Several of these poems are maps to a land that Robinson has made his own and we think of them whenever we think of lives blocked off before their due date. Robinson is unequaled in the presentation of this land. In Shaw's play *Heartbreak*

House Effie cries out for "life with a blessing!" and Shaw would give it if he could, but the bombs fall and Effie welcomes them. There are no bombs in Robinson's poems, no apocalypses, and few blessings. In those poems blessings are things that have been or never were. In "Veteran Sirens" Robinson says, "Poor flesh, to fight the calendar so long!" and this is a common burden in these poems. "The Unforgiven" is one of the greatest in this line:

> When he, who is the unforgiven,
> Beheld her first, he found her fair:
> No promise ever dreamt in heaven
> Could then have lured him anywhere
> That would have been away from there;
> And all his wits had lightly striven,
> Foiled with her voice, and eyes, and hair.
>
> There's nothing in the saints and sages
> To meet the shafts her glances had,
> Or such as hers have had for ages
> To blind a man till he be glad,
> And humble him till he be mad.
> The story would have many pages,
> And would be neither good nor bad.
>
> And, having followed, you would find him
> Where properly the play begins;
> But look for no red light behind him—
> No fumes of many-colored sins,
> Fanned high by screaming violins.
> God knows what good it was to blind him,
> Or whether man or woman wins.
>
> And by the same eternal token,
> Who knows just how it will all end?—
> This drama of hard words unspoken,
> This fireside farce, without a friend
> Or enemy to comprehend
> What augurs when two lives are broken,
> And fear finds nothing left to mend.
>
> He stares in vain for what awaits him,
> And sees in Love a coin to toss;

He smiles, and her cold hush berates him
Beneath his hard half of the cross;
They wonder why it ever was;
And she, the unforgiving, hates him
More for her lack than for her loss.

He feeds with pride his indecision,
And shrinks from what will not occur,
Bequeathing with infirm derision
His ashes to the days that were,
Before she made him prisoner;
And labors to retrieve the vision
That he must once have had of her.

He waits, and there awaits an ending,
And he knows neither what nor when;
But no magicians are attending
To make him see as he saw then,
And he will never find again
The face that once had been the rending
Of all his purpose among men.

He blames her not, nor does he chide her,
And she has nothing new to say;
If he were Bluebeard he could hide her,
But that's not written in the play,
And there will be no change today;
Although, to the serene outsider,
There still would seem to be a way.

We cannot set this aside as one of life's little ironies. It cannot even be disposed of as a domestic tragedy, because there is, literally, no conflict, no drama at all. Indeed, this is how the two lives are defined—by invoking several forms of drama in which these people could not now play a part. They are held as in a faded photograph, a fireside scene without the splendor of fire. They could not be pushed into a classical tragedy though one might think of them if one were casting a play by Samuel Beckett. Indeed, like Beckett's characters, they are people to whom something once happened; they have had, presumably, "happy days" and now they know with a terrible certainty that the Lord does not hold up "all that fall." This is the point of the last stanza: these people are not only beyond praise or blame, they are beyond speech itself, like Krapp at the end of *Krapp's Last Tape*. Far from being the victims of tragedy, they could not now play a part in a Bluebeard melodrama. And the serene outsiders—you and I—shake our heads and think that perhaps we, like love, could find a way.

Many of Robinson's best poems work along these lines. Like the Wall in *A Midsummer Night's Dream*, they say, "the truth is so." And the truth is normally set down in a house, a village, a cage, in which people are transfixed. Harry Monchonsey in *The Family Reunion* castigates his aunts and uncles for being people to whom nothing has happened. In many of Robinson's poems they would be featured almost as happy folk. Robinson's characters still cling to the metaphor of action because they have nothing else to do. Their suffering is caused by the fact that, for them, the reality upon which the dramatic metaphor depends is dead. Such words as *decision, choice, do, event,* or *act* are their only terms of reference, and these terms are—for these people—dead.

Another remarkable poem in this way is "The Poor Relation." I give two stanzas, the third and fourth of nine:

> To those who come for what she was—
> The few left who know where to find her—
> She clings, for they are all she has;
> And she may smile when they remind her,
> As heretofore, of what they know
> Of roses that are still to blow
> By ways where not so much as grass
> Remains of what she sees behind her.
>
> They stay awhile, and having done
> What penance or the past requires,
> They go, and leave her there alone
> To count her chimneys and her spires.
> Her lip shakes when they go away,
> And yet she would not have them stay;
> She knows as well as anyone
> That Pity, having played, soon tires.

So pity is a fractious child, if not a naked, newborn babe, and an afternoon visit to a faded relative is strenuous play with little in the way of amuse-

ment. This is perhaps as sharp as we like poetic tones to be. What sustains
the poem is that Robinson is scrupulously just to the occasion. He has no
interest in setting the table with well-placed ironies; his object is—in Yeats's
phrase—to hold reality and justice in a single thought.

Another fine poem in this genre is "Aaron Stark," and here the search
for reality and justice is directed to keep pity in its place. Indeed, this is
common in Robinson's poems. If his characters break their lives and waste
them in their cages, if life itself is pitiless, at least he will not have its victims
humiliated by your pity or mine. If his people are isolated, he will leave
them their privacy; he will not have it smeared by affluent offers of good
will. Nor will he turn his little men into heroes to assuage our guilt:

> Withal a meagre man was Aaron Stark,
> Cursed and unkempt, shrewd, shrivelled, and morose.
> A miser was he, with a miser's nose,
> And eyes like little dollars in the dark.
> His thin, pinched mouth was nothing but a mark;
> And when he spoke there came like sullen blows
> Through scattered fangs a few snarled words and close,
> As if a cur were chary of its bark.
>
> Glad for the murmur of his hard renown,
> Year after year he shambled through the town,
> A loveless exile moving with a staff;
> And oftentimes there crept into his ears
> A sound of alien pity, touched with tears,—
> And then (and only then) did Aaron laugh.

Our response is changed, almost word by word. "Meagre" is neutral so far,
and if "unkempt" brings out the beast of sympathy, we are meant to stiffen
again with "shrewd" and "morose," and to continue hard with the snarling
words and blows. But our sympathy is again enlisted for the figure sham-
bling through the town, and especially for the loveless exile with a stick,
who sounds like someone from *Pilgrim's Progress*—so much so that the pity
Aaron hears is our pity, the tears are our tears. And only then does Robinson give him the last laugh, although this will serve no purpose except to
reassert the claims of a justice poetic if not real.

Life broken against the cage of circumstance, where circumstance is
featured as the malice of things and often embodied in another person—a
husband, a wife—is Robinson's land of broken images. He doesn't blame

God for it as insistently as Thomas Hardy does; his pages are not as relentlessly marked off by those capitalized enemies who, in Hardy's poems, work for a malignant deity. Robinson took possession of those images, I think, with some ease. The difficulties poured in upon him when he went one stage further, featuring the malice of things within the individual self, the single state of man divided against itself. And of all the forms of division the crucial one in Robinson's poems is that suggested by the juxtaposition of reason and passion. Robinson was engrossed with this problem in some of his best and some of his worst poems. The worst we can tolerate if we think of them now as no more than notebooks in which he made random jottings for his great theme, turning them into verse in a spare hour.

"Demos and Dionysus" is a case in point. It is as bad as a poem can be that is a versified notebook, but it has the interest of a rough draft on a major theme. Demos and Dionysus argue at some length about the forces that we would think of today as totalitarianism and personalism. Demos is the spokesman of reason, the machine age, the elimination of personality. He tells us that in his Kingdom Come the recalcitrant will be "rationed into reason." And of course he is in all this a parody of that reason on which many would pin their hopes. Demos will promise us an administered paradise, a passionless state. Dionysus asks, reasonably enough, "What will be left in your millennium / When self and soul are gone and all subdued / Insensibly?" And the argument drags its slow length along until Dionysus invokes a higher kind of reason, which we can call (though he does not) imagination. He says to Demos:

> I mean, also,
> An increment of reason not like yours,
> Which is the crucifixion of all reason,
> But one that quickens in the seed of truth,
> And is the flower of truth—not always fair,
> Yet always to be found if you will see it.
> There *is* a Demos, and you know his name
> By force of easy stealing; yet his face
> Would be one of a melancholy stranger
> To you if he saw yours.

It is not an engaging description, I am afraid, and it amounts to little more than the assertion that man in the fullness of time will live by the justice of his imagination rather than by "reason's click clack"—as Stevens calls it. The truth of imagination will set us free and make us whole.

A better parable on the same theme is the poem "Maya":

Through an ascending emptiness of night,
Leaving the flesh and the complacent mind
Together in their sufficiency behind,
The soul of man went up to a far height;
And where those others would have had no sight
Or sense of else than terror for the blind,
Soul met the Will, and was again consigned
To the supreme illusion which is right.

"And what goes on up there," the Mind inquired,
"That I know not already to be true?"—
"More than enough, but not enough for you,"
Said the descending Soul: "Here in the dark,
Where you are least revealed when most admired,
You may still be the bellows and the spark."

The logic will not stand much pressure, but at least the poem is pushing the problem a little nearer to the terms in which it will be usefully defined— terms of order and chaos, and the minuscule orders that are no answer to chaos at all but merely beg the question. But the very least the poem affirms is that the mind's typical fault is complacency, unless it is prepared to go beyond its own comforts, at which point it becomes imagination, its better self.

The best poem, however, on the theme of passion and reason is "New England," one of Robinson's most controlled achievements:

Here where the wind is always north-north-east
And children learn to walk on frozen toes,
Wonder begets an envy of all those
Who boil elsewhere with such a lyric yeast
Of love that you will hear them at a feast
Where demons would appeal for some repose,
Still clamoring where the chalice overflows
And crying wildest who have drunk the least.

Passion is here a soilure of the wits,
We're told, and Love a cross for them to bear;
Joy shivers in the corner where she knits
And Conscience always has the rocking-chair,
Cheerful as when she tortured into fits
The first cat that was ever killed by Care.

The lines are drawn very sharply here, but not so sharply as to be unjust or merely melodramatic. The images of constriction lead almost immediately into their extreme opposite, images of riot, *la dolce vita*. There is no sense in which the second images offer a serious alternative to the first, nor is Robinson putting them forward in that way. They are as "wrong" as the situation that compelled them, the nearest possibility of the human spirit when all the central imaginative possibilities have been constricted. One of the remarkable qualities of the poem is the control exhibited in the sudden change from the dramatic scene of riot to the mime of New England theory at the beginning of the sestet: "Passion is here a soilure of the wits, / We're told." This prepares the way for the representation of joy and conscience as allegorical emblems, figures in a moral triptych. They are presented without movement, because movement implies an open situation of possibility and these two live in a world of morally constricting finalities long since established. They are the guardians of the law—in T. S. Eliot's phrase—and they reflect their master with daunting exactitude. Indeed, we have to think of them, since Robinson invented them, as the kind of people who inhabit several of his own narratives. Make conscience male and joy female and we have the synopsis of several bleak poems from his own country. In any event, the poem sets up its own values—ease, freedom, nonchalance, possibility—and the kinds of passion, love, joy, and conscience that those values would entertain.

In the long narratives love is often a cross for hero and heroine to bear, but it is sometimes more than that. In the third book of *Tristram* Isolt of Ireland comes to her lover:

> Came nearer still to him and still said nothing,
> Till terror born of passion became passion
> Reborn of terror while his lips and hers
> Put speech out like a flame put out by fire.

Isolt tries to console Tristram, and in one particularly lovely passage she says:

> Something in you was always in my father:
> A darkness always was around my father,
> Since my first eyes remembered him. He saw
> Nothing, but he would see the shadow of it
> Before he saw the color or shape it had,
> Or where the sun was. Tristram, fair things yet
> Will have a shadow black as night before them,

> And soon will have a shadow black as night
> Behind them. And all this may be shadow,
> Sometime, that we may live to see behind us—

And when she speaks of her love, "larger than all time and all places," she contrasts it with the normal, temporal loves in which the violence is subdued to a puny order. She says:

> I do not think there is much love like ours
> Here in this life, or that too much of it
> Would make poor men and women who go alone
> Into their graves without it more content.
> Or more by common sorrow to be envied
> Than they are now. This may be true, or not.
> Perhaps I am not old enough to know—
> Not having lived always, nor having seen
> Much else than everything disorderly
> Deformed to order into a small court,
> Where love was most a lie.

This is Isolt's theme, and it is one version of Robinson's—the easy, puny formula that replaces the genuine form, the tiny orders that cut down to size the passions that are the substance of all orders, and their justification. This is where the best of Robinson is to be found. He dramatized for modern American poets one of the problems of a perennial ethics. Some poets see it as the conflict between reason and passion, others as that between authority and the self. I want to think of two poets in this context, and say a little about them, before coming back to Robinson.

The first poet is J. V. Cunningham, generally considered a poet of intellectual rigor, who delights in exact statements, concepts, sentences, resilient surfaces. And this is true. If there must be a war between reason and passion, or rather, if one of the perennial wars must be defined in those intolerably simple terms, then he will enlist for reason. Indeed, many of his poems have seemed to offer readers the comfort of feeling that the firm mind, even yet, can control disheveled and violent experience. This is not, I think, the moral of his story, but it is often implied in his poems. In "The Beacon," for instance, he says:

> Men give their hearts away;
> Whether for good or ill
>   They cannot say
> Who shape the object in their will.

The will in pure delight
Conceives itself. I praise
    Far lamps at night,
Cold landmarks for reflection's gaze.

Distant they still remain,
Oh, unassailed, apart!
    May time attain
The promise ere death seals the heart!

This is to say—as Cunningham has said it—that since so many of our desires are functions of our will—objects made by the will in its own likeness—we should try to deceive the will by interposing a safe distance between ourselves and the object, so that its otherness will be secured. We can then contemplate the object intransitively, and if time relents, we may even come to possess it.

Cunningham allows that this is a desperate expedient. Nor will it secure for us a unified life. Far from it. A man must live, Cunningham says, "divided against himself: only the selfishly insane can integrate experience to the heart's desire, and only the emotionally sterile would not wish to." For one thing, there is the fact that one's primary experience is absolute. "What is is, and even this is to say too much." Hence the great achievement would be to integrate the subjectivity of passion with the objectivity of reason, thereby altering both as in a dramatic conflict. For the poet—although Cunningham does not use these terms—this would involve the grappling of opposites; in Coleridge's terms, more than usual emotion with more than usual order. Or in Wallace Stevens's terms, it would be a conflict of two violences, within and without.

When Cunningham speaks of the obstacles to the clear light of reason, he allows for several, including spiritual pride and that area of irrational experience that he symbolizes as the dusk. There is also necessity. And there is passion. In regard to necessity, a man is conditioned by the nature of his awareness. He lives only to accept and to adjust himself to the brutal fulfillment of his insight in the outer world. It follows that "all choice is error," for choice implies "exclusion, rejection, restriction, limitation." This doctrine is closely related to another, the idea of evil as a defect of being. Cunningham interprets this very severely and, I think, goes far beyond the philosophical texts he might offer in his support. He says:

Any realised particular, anything which is this and not that and that, is by the very fact evil. For to be this is to exclude not only any other alternative but to exclude all else in the universe. Perfection is in possibility, in the idea, but that which is realised, specific, determined, has no possibilities. It is precisely this and nothing else at all. It is lacking in all the being of the universe other than its own particularity. The more realised a thing is the greater its defect of being; hence any particular choice is as such evil though morally it may be the best choice.

I should disagree with this on the grounds that a tulip cannot be said to lack anything in not being an elephant. The quality of being is embodied in particular existents, things that *are*. A thing is defective only if it does not realize its individuating form. A particular woman cannot be said to be defective because there are millions of women not she. Cunningham says that the problem, as he has defined it, is certainly central, "and very likely insoluble":

> For it is not merely philosophy but one's life. If [one] accepts the classic solution in which choice is thought of as the inevitable result in action of reasoned and considered judgment, then choice is completely determined in such fashion that the moral agent may be assured he has inescapably moved toward the best. . . . It is true that in classical ethics the rightness of right reason is considered to be constantly imperilled by passion, against which one must be unremittingly and warily on guard. But the consequence of this position is to enforce an absolute dualism of reason and passion, unmanageable except, perhaps, by religious and ritual means.

The only way out, it would seem, is to go ahead and choose, and then protect oneself against the exorbitance of the choice.

Cunningham has written very few poems that are not involved in this dilemma in some way or other. But two poems seem to me particularly important in its development, a short poem, "August Hail," and a long one, the recent and very remarkable sequence called "To What Strangers? What Welcome?"

The subject of the first, "August Hail," was, he tells us, "the sudden incidence of passion, which comes like an impersonal force and apparently from the outside":

> In late summer the wild geese
> In the white draws are flying.
> The grain beards in the blue peace.

> The weeds are drying.
> The hushed sky breeds hail.
> Who shall revenge unreason?
> Wheat headless in the white flail
> Denies the season.

By giving the situation in meteorological terms, so that unreason comes as hail, Cunningham evades the ethical problem, more or less as Marvell in his "Horatian Ode" evades the problem of judging Cromwell's actions by speaking of them as bursts of lightning, natural events that do not raise an ethical problem, since they are not caused by man. But it is strange to find Cunningham, who is normally severe with the unreason of others, writing in an escape clause here that would make us all innocent. In "To What Strangers? What Welcome?" the issue comes up again in a much more problematic setting.

The new sequence has a very simple plot: a man travels west, falls in love, and comes back. The poems begin with an epigraph from Robinson's long poem *Merlin,* the seventh book, where Merlin leaves Vivian and returns to Camelot. It is worth mentioning, perhaps, that Merlin's speech also evades the ethical issue by positing a neutral curve of events in which he is implicated. "In Broceliande," he tells Dagonet, "Time overtook me as I knew he must." And a few lines further, in a passage that Cunningham omits, Merlin says:

> I shall not go back.
> We pay for going back; and all we get
> Is one more needless ounce of weary wisdom
> To bring away with us.

And even if he doesn't go back, Vivian will understand and say:

> Time called him home,
> And that was as it was; for much is lost
> Between Broceliande and Camelot.

(It is, as Cunningham knows, one of Robinson's most beautiful passages.)

The sequence consists of fifteen very short poems, some of only four lines, others about twelve or fifteen. It would be pleasant to go through the poems now, line by line, but I must jump over many lovely lines and passages to settle upon those nearest my theme—the tenth poem, for instance, after the falling in love:

A half hour for coffee, and at night
An hour or so of unspoken speech,
Hemming a summer dress as the tide
Turns at the right time.

                                             Must it be sin,
This consummation of who knows what?
This sharp cry at entrance, once, and twice?
This unfulfilled fulfilment?

                              Something
That happens because it must happen.
We live in the given. Consequence,
And lack of consequence, both fail us.
Good is what we can do with evil.

When I read this for the first time I thought it exhibited a weary determin-
ism, almost a version of Manicheanism, which I found disturbing. Cunningham has argued against the reading, saying that the statements are
"simply human; more concerned with sorting the experience of a particular
context than with espousing the History of Ideas." So we must take the
statements in the first instance as dramatic expressions of the moment. If
they were to be offered as anything more—as doctrine, for instance—they
would still seem to me slack, especially the dissolution of an "act" until it
becomes a mere happening. In either event, it seems necessary to interpret
"evil" in Cunningham's special sense as "defect of being," a certain innate
paucity of "the given." And the sequence ends:

                    Identity, that spectator
                    Of what he calls himself, that net
                    And aggregate of energies
                    In transient combination—some
                    So marginal are they mine? Or is
                    There mine? I sit in the last warmth
                    Of a New England fall, and I?
                    A premise of identity
                    Where the lost hurries to be lost,
                    Both in its own best interests
                    And in the interests of life.

That is, the narrator, after his experience of passion, is struck by what Cunningham elsewhere calls "the indeterminable sources of personal identity,"

the void region of possibilities whose principle of being is to be neither this nor that. Love, "the allegiance of passion to a given external object," betrays this inner void, forces it to yield up one of those multitudinous possibilities. Hence the effect of the experience has been to break up the tight order of energies that traded under the narrator's name. The new order—when it comes—will be different, because the emergence of that possibility from the void into the light of historical day changes the old configuration. At the moment the narrator is only "a premise of identity," as if he had not yet quite emerged from the "dusk" of things.

I have, of course, neglected nearly all those qualities in Cunningham's sequence that make it one of the most beautiful of modern poems—the scrupulous rigor, the finesse of cadence, the sturdiness and variety of the images. But I have wanted to make one point: in Cunningham's new poems the theme of reason and passion—which we isolated in Robinson's work—is extended and dramatized with the greatest resilience. Far from arranging skirmishes between reason and passion and fixing the fights in reason's behalf, Cunningham is offering reason a more stringent challenge than any available in contemporary poetry. In the poem "Socrates" Yvor Winters speaks of the mind of Athens surpassing the flux, "when tongue and stone subside, her thought be sure." We hope it will. And in a recent poem Winters says that passion running undefined "may ruin what the masters taught." And we know it will. One part of Cunningham's achievement is to dramatize the unpredictable run of passion, so that we can the better understand it, even if we cannot anticipate its next veering. And to stand for all the poetry I have ignored, I quote without comment the eighth poem in this new sequence:

> The night is still. The unfailing surf
> In passion and subsidence moves
> As at a distance. The glass walls,
> And redwood, are my utmost being,
> And is there, there in the last shadow,
> There in the final privacies
> Of unaccosted grace,—is there,
> Gracing the tedium to death,
> An intimation? Something much
> Like love, like loneliness adrowse
> In states more primitive than peace,
> In the warm wonder of winter sun.

The second poet who seems to me distinctly relevant is Robert Lowell. His poems have been offered to us, over the years, in several contexts. For

a few years we were advised to consider him a major Catholic poet, and
this gave us—depending upon our attitude to Catholicism—either a stick
with which to beat the poems or a pilgrim's staff to help us reach them.
Either way it was a temporary facility. We have also been told to think of
the poems, especially the early ones in *Lord Weary's Castle,* as acts of violence directed against all the forces of constriction wherever the poet feels
them—especially those associated with his own New England ancestors,
guardians of a deadly law. This has now become critical orthodoxy in regard to Lowell's poems, and we tend to grasp it, on the principle that rec-
ommends any port in a storm. But I think we have settled down too easily.
It is not very difficult to make a few generalizations about the New England
ancestors, accurate or not, but there is very little evidence in the poems to
support the sentimental image of a tender poet wounded and darkened by
his membership in a great dark family. The occasions that incite those
poems are invariably immediate, personal; we don't need to go back to
Plymouth Rock.

In fact, I would suggest that the crucial theme in Lowell's poems—
authority and the self—is a variant of Robinson's theme, reason and passion, and that the proper context in which to consider it is the context
defined by Robinson. Teased out a little it amounts to this: the individual
self can rely upon its own resources—such as they are—or it can accept the
order provided for it by a compelling, totalitarian force, of whatever kind,
or it can spend a lifetime searching for a more benign, more personal order,
sufficiently firm to make its edicts persuasive if not legal. If the self refuses
all external orders and trusts in its own direction, it runs the risk of expo-
sure, loneliness, a terrible desiccation of spirit, utter chaos. There are several
figures of this kind in Lowell's poems, notably the heroine of "Katherine's
Dream" and the husband in "To Speak of the Woe That Is in Marriage," the
husband who "hits the streets to cruise for prostitutes." And the condition
itself is generalized in "Christmas Eve under Hooker's Statue" as "our fields
are running wild." In "Colloquy in Black Rock" it is given in these lines:

> My heart, you race and stagger and demand
> More blood-gangs for your nigger-brass percussions,
> Till I, the stunned machine of your devotion,
> Clanging upon this cymbal of a hand,
> Am rattled screw and footloose.

If the self takes the first opportunity of coming in out of the storm, it
is likely to come upon an authoritarian order, and the price of this shelter
is the attenuation of the self until he becomes the no-man favored by all

authoritarian states. In Lowell's poems this force is offered in several forms: as "lion-taming Satan" in "The Ferris Wheel"; once as Mammon; sometimes as the narrator's father; once as "my cold-eyed fathers"; once as God; once as Hooker in the poem "Christmas Eve under Hooker's Statue," where he speaks of "the long horn of plenty" breaking like glass in Hooker's gauntlets; and once as Herod in the poem "The Holy Innocents." Indeed, this poem is perhaps the clearest version of the parable: Herod is the totalitarian order, the grip of claw, and the lovely alternative is Christ, whose order is sweet and gracious. But the world in 1945 knows only Herod, so the self, the spirit, suffers:

> Listen, the hay-bells tinkle as the cart
> Wavers on rubber tires along the tar
> And cindered ice below the burlap mill
> And ale-wife run. The oxen drool and start
> In wonder at the fenders of a car,
> And blunder hugely up St. Peter's hill.
> These are the undefiled by woman—their
> Sorrow is not the sorrow of this world:
> King Herod shrieking vengeance at the curled
> Up knees of Jesus choking in the air,
>
> A king of speechless clods and infants. Still
> The world out-Herods Herod; and the year,
> The nineteen-hundred forty-fifth of grace,
> Lumbers with losses up the clinkered hill
> Of our purgation; and the oxen near
> The worn foundations of their resting-place,
> The holy manger where their bed is corn
> And holly torn for Christmas. If they die,
> Ah Jesus, in the harness, who will mourn?
> Lamb of the Shepherds, Child, how still you lie.

And then, sometimes, there is a benign order. In Robert Lowell's autobiographical poems this order is often embodied in his grandfather, especially in the poem "Grandparents" in *Life Studies*. In the Christian poems it is figured in Christian emblems, as for instance the crucifix in the poem "Concord," set off against "Mammon's unbridled industry." In many of these poems it is Christ himself, often the object of prayer. In the poem "Adam and Eve" the narrator says:

> They lied,
> My cold-eyed seedy fathers when they died,
> Or rather threw their lives away, to fix
> Sterile, forbidding nameplates on the bricks
> Above a kettle. Jesus rest their souls!

In "Colloquy in Black Rock" the enabling image is the kingfisher, probably a half-echo from a poem by Hopkins, and it brings the fire of Christ:

> Christ walks on the black water. In Black Mud
> Darts the kingfisher. On Corpus Christi, heart,
> Over the drum-beat of St. Stephen's choir
> I hear him, *Stupor Mundi,* and the mud
> Flies from his hunching wings and beak—my heart,
> The blue kingfisher dives on you in fire.

Religious belief apart, Christ was a fitting symbol of a new order for this poet, because he contained within himself the knowledge of blood and violence. It would be, in the highest degree, a personal order, not predatory or aggressive. This is why the last stanza of the poem "New Year's Day" is so important:

> Under St. Peter's bell the parish sea
>
> Swells with its smelt into the burlap shack
> Where Joseph plucks his hand-lines like a harp,
> And hears the fearful *Puer natus est*
> Of Circumcision, and relives the wrack
> And howls of Jesus whom he holds. How sharp
> The burden of the Law before the beast:
> Time and the grindstone and the knife of God.
> The Child is born in blood, O child of blood.

And all of this is implied in the poem "Our Lady of Walsingham." Indeed, the motto that we might use as a way in to those poems in *Lord Weary's Castle* is the line of prophecy—"and the world shall come to Walsingham." Within our terms of reference we could give it a prose translation somewhat like this: The world's order, which shows every proof of out-Heroding Herod and going many steps further in the grip of claw, will one day give up its murderous cruelty and take to the benign order of Walsingham. And Lowell describes Our Lady of Walsingham thus:

> Our Lady, too small for her canopy,
> Sits near the altar. There's no comeliness
> At all or charm in that expressionless
> Face with its heavy eyelids. As before,
> This face, for centuries a memory,
> *Non est species, neque decor,*
> Expressionless, expresses God: it goes
> Past castled Sion. She knows what God knows,
> Not Calvary's Cross nor crib at Bethlehem
> Now, and the world shall come to Walsingham.

If it appears that this new order involves the obliteration of self, some—like T. S. Eliot—would be prepared to accept this, and others would regard the price as exorbitant. But I think we have to read the lines more carefully, and think of them not quite in doctrinal terms. There is a passage in Yeats, in "The Trembling of the Veil," which throws light on this. Yeats has been discussing a certain type of person who must not seek an image of desire but must await that which lies beyond his mind—"unities not of the mind, but unities of Nature, unities of God." Such people, Yeats says, must "hollow their hearts till they are void and without form," must "become the lamp for another's wick and oil." Lowell's version is, "Expressionless, expresses God." And of course if she knows what God knows, she knows the fury and the mire of human veins. So the self is not obliterated; it is transfigured, rather.

If reason and passion—the "antinomies of day and night," as Yeats calls them—are given in this form, then the isolated self is all passion, and reason is the authoritative order, either gentle or rough, Christ or Herod. Where the only available order is authoritarian, totalitarian, the self will squirm and cower, or it will yield. Some of Lowell's most remarkable poems are written to dramatize this situation, where there is no middle term, no gentle order, no Christ, and no hope of finding him, and the self cowers before an angry God. The finest poem in this group is "Mr. Edwards and the Spider," in which Lowell uses the persona of Jonathan Edwards. We are to think of Edwards meditating upon God and man as the tiger and the spider. The material of the poem is largely taken from Edwards's boyhood essay on insects and his famous sermon "Sinners in the Hands of an Angry God." In the early essay Edwards observed the habits of spiders moving to their death in the sea. In the sermon he gave a terrifying picture of God holding us over the pit of Hell as He would a spider. We are held above the pit, at every moment, only by God's arbitrary will and pleasure. (I think the difficulties of the poem are eased somewhat if we take it as a letter written by Edwards to the elder Joseph Hawley. This man, thrown into despair as a result of Edwards's sermons, cut his throat and died on June 1, 1735.) The poem reads:

> I saw the spiders marching through the air,
> Swimming from tree to tree that mildewed day
>   In latter August when the hay
>   Came creaking to the Barn. But where
>   The wind is westerly,
>   Where gnarled November makes the spiders fly
>   Into the apparitions of the sky,
>   They purpose nothing but their ease and die
> Urgently beating east to sunrise and the sea;
>
>   What are we in the hands of the great God?
>   It was in vain you set up thorn and briar
>   In battle array against the fire
>   And treason crackling in your blood;
>   F the wild thorns grow tame
>   And will do nothing to oppose the flame;
>   Your lacerations tell the losing game
>   You play against a sickness past your cure.
> How will the hands be strong? How will the heart endure?
>
>   A very little thing, a little worm,
>   Or hourglass-blazoned spider, it is said,
>   Can kill a tiger. Will the dead
>   Hold up his mirror and affirm
>   To the four winds the smell
>   And flash of his authority? It's well
>   If God who holds you to the pit of hell,
>   Much as one holds a spider, will destroy,
>   Baffle and dissipate your soul. As a small boy
>
> On Windsor Marsh, I saw the spider die
> When thrown into the bowels of fierce fire:
>   There's no long struggle, no desire
>   To get up on its feet and fly—
>   It stretches out its feet

And dies. This is the sinner's last retreat;
Yes, and no strength exerted on the heat
Then sinews the abolished will, when sick
And full of burning, it will whistle on a brick.

But who can plumb the sinking of that soul?
Josiah Hawley, picture yourself cast
   Into a brick-kiln where the blast
   Fans your quick vitals to a coal—
     If measured by a glass,
How long would it seem burning! Let there pass
A minute, ten, ten trillion; but the blaze
   Is infinite, eternal: this is death,
To die and know it. This is the Black Widow, death.

Edwards is speaking on behalf of an angry God. Hawley is the recalcitrant self, setting up thorn and briar against the "fire and treason" in his blood, perhaps still hoping for the intervention of a benign force with benign images. But Edwards specifically excludes the possibility; the sickness is past cure. And he demands that Hawley confront the truth of the angry God in its authoritarian force, directly, without mediation. In "Sinners in the Hands of an Angry God" he says: "You hang by a slender thread, with the flames of divine wrath flashing about it, and ready every moment to singe it, and burn it asunder; and you have no interest in any Mediator, and nothing to lay hold of to save yourself, nothing to keep off the flames of wrath, nothing of your own, nothing that you ever have done, nothing that you can do, to induce God to spare you one moment." The third stanza of the poem is rather dark. A little thing, a worm, an infection of some kind, shall we say, can kill a tiger. But if the literal tiger can be killed, not so the God-tiger. Will the dead, the poem asks, hold up an image of the tiger and affirm its authority? Perhaps not. But have no doubt about the smell and flash of that other tiger, God, and his authority. If God chooses to destroy you, well and good; thus justice is served. In the sermon Edwards says: 'They deserve to be cast into hell; so that divine justice never stands in the way, it makes no objection against God's using his power at any moment to destroy them. Yea, on the contrary, justice calls aloud for an infinite punishment of their sins. Divine justice says of the tree that brings forth such grapes of Sodom, 'Cut it down, why cumbereth it the ground?' "

I am arguing, of course, that this poem dramatizes one of the crucial positions in Lowell's theme, authority and the self. If you set up two terms and hope for the disclosure of a saving third, there must be a stern voice that denies this hope and challenges the self on behalf of a totalitarian God. This voice will have to reckon with others, hence the dialectic of Lowell's poems will canvass all the possibilities. And I am also arguing, of course, that it is better to read the poems in this way than to take them as issuing from his special position as a member of the Lowell family. They are wider in ramification, more general in scope. The search for a mediator between the self and a totalitarian authority is still proceeding in the recent verse plays and the recent poems.

In Robinson's case there was a resolution, of a kind. And it is to be found in the long poems. In *Tristram* after the hero's death Isolt lives with her dreams. *Lancelot* ends with the hero "Not knowing what last havoc pity and love / Had still to wreak on wisdom." Guinevere will not go with him, and he goes away alone, but a voice tells him that "a world has died / For you, that a world may live." And as he rides away he sees what he has always sought, the gleam, the light. The same vision is granted to Archibald in the poem "Isaac and Archibald," "a light behind the stars." *Merlin* ends with darkness over Camelot and Merlin's vision of "two fires that are to light the world." And on the last page of the *Collected Poems* the destruction of King Jasper's kingdom is witnessed by its sole survivor, Zoë:

> She was hearing
> Crashes and rumblings in the house behind her
> That she had left; and over her shoulder now,
> She could see flame within that filled the windows
> With more than fire and light.

Indeed the difference between Robinson's heroic narratives and the shorter poems, length apart, is that the legends offered him a release from the furies of reason and passion; sometimes a new dawn, sometimes an apocalyptic flame, often a gleam, a light. In the short poems, the poems of circumstance, there was often no way out. The Arthurian legends, halfway between time and eternity, gave him a visionary gleam that he could not find on earth and would not posit there. That was why he needed them.

There was another reason. He wanted to give his characters room to move and he thought he could not do so in the modern poetic world. Indeed, he offers little or nothing in the modern way of poetry; no gargoyles of memorable phrase, no startling juxtapositions. Robinson is a poet as Hardy is a poet, putting most of his capital in people, places, things. But Robinson's best poems are finer than Hardy's, because Hardy's poems are invariably a little innocent, they think they have found the answer when they have barely defined the question. Robinson trusted his answers for truth but not for current application; the modern world would always evade them, making them look archaic. So much the worse. He would persist, composing thousands of words to prove against Yeats that words alone are not "certain good." The "good" resides in human events, people, modes of being, action and suffering: the poet's task is to understand. This is the "tradition" embodied in poems as different in other respects as Robinson's "Eros Turannos" and Wordsworth's "The Old Cumberland Beggar"; masterpieces, both.

JAMES DICKEY

Edwin Arlington Robinson: The Many Truths

A reevaluation of the work of a poet as established as Edwin Arlington Robinson should involve us in some of the fundamentals we tend to forget when we read any poetry that happens to come to hand—the poetry that is thrust upon us by critics and in courses in literature as well as the poetry that we seek out or return to. As should be true of our encounter with any poetry, reevaluation requires that we rid ourselves of preconceptions and achieve, if we can, a way of reading an established poet as though we had never heard of him and were opening his book for the first time. It requires that we approach him with all our senses open, our intelligence in acute readiness, our critical sense in check but alert for the slightest nuance of falsity, our truth-sensitive needle—the device that measures what the poet says against what we know from having lived it—at its most delicate, and our sense of the poet's "place," as determined by commentary, textbook, and literary fashion, drugged, asleep, or temporarily dead.

Like most ideal conditions, this one cannot be fully attained. But it is certainly true that an approximation of such a state is both an advantage and a condition productive of unsuspected discoveries in reading poets we thought we knew, particularly poets whom we thought we knew as well as Robinson. In Robinson's special case it is even more difficult than usual, for the course of poetry has to a certain extent turned away from him, making his greatest virtues appear mediocre ones and directing public scrutiny from his introspective, intellectual, and ironic verse toward poetry in which more things seem to be taking place in a smaller area—poetry in which the poetic

From *Selected Poems of Edwin Arlington Robinson,* edited by Morton Dauwen Zabel. © 1965 by the Macmillan Publishing Co.

line is compressed and packed to the point of explosion and the bedazzle-
ment of the reader is considered synonymous with his reward.

Robinson achieved unusual popularity in his lifetime. When he died in
1935, at the age of sixty-five, he had won the Pulitzer Prize three times and
had gained a distinction rare for a poet—his book-length poem *Tristram*
had become a best-seller. But in the public mind, Robinson has during recent years been regarded as only his vices of prolixity, irresolution, and
occasional dullness would have him. Yet if we could manage to read Robinson as if we did not know him—or at least as if we did not know him
quite so well as we had believed—or if we could come to him as if he were
worth rereading, not out of duty and obedience to literary history but as a
possible experience, we would certainly gain a good deal more than we
would lose.

I

Suppose, eager only for the experience of poems, we were to look
through this book before reading it, noting only the shapes of the poems on
the page. We would see a good many short, tight-looking poems in different
structural forms, all of them severely symmetrical, and page after page con-
taining long vertical rectangles of blank verse. Though this selection leaves
out the Arthurian poems on which Robinson's popular reputation was
made as well as the other later narratives of his declining years, there are
still a number of middling-long poems that no editor interested in Robinson's best work could possibly eliminate. The chances are that we would be
inclined to skip these and first read one of the shorter ones. What would we
find if it were this one?

> We go no more to Calverly's,
> For there the lights are few and low;
> And who are there to see by them,
> Or what they see, we do not know.
> Poor strangers of another tongue
> May now creep in from anywhere,
> And we, forgotten, be no more
> Than twilight on a ruin there.
>
> We two, the remnant. All the rest
> Are cold and quiet. You nor I,
> Nor fiddle now, nor flagon-lid,

May ring them back from where they lie.
No fame delays oblivion
For them, but something yet survives:
A record written fair, could we
But read the book of scattered lives.

There'll be a page for Leffingwell,
And one for Lingard, the Moon-calf;
And who knows what for Clavering,
Who died because he couldn't laugh?
Who knows or cares? No sign is here,
No face, no voice, no memory;
No Lingard with his eerie joy,
No Clavering, no Calverly.

We cannot have them here with us
To say where their light lives are gone,
Or if they be of other stuff
Than are the moons of Ilion.
So, be their place of one estate
With ashes, echoes, and old wars—
Or ever we be of the night,
Or we be lost among the stars.

It is a poem that opens, conventionally enough, with a reference to a place—one suspects from the beginning that it is one of those drinking places where men gather against the dark and call it fellowship—where there were once parties or at least conviviality of some sort; of that company, only two are left, and one of these is speaking. We feel the conventionality of the theme because we are aware that the contrast between places formerly full of animation and merriment with the same places *now* is one of the most haggard of romantic clichés and the subject of innumerable mediocre verses (though infrequently, as in some of Hardy, it can be memorable and can serve to remind us that such contrasts, such places, do in fact exist and *are* melancholy and cautionary). Yet there is a difference, a departure, slight but definitive, from the conventional. This difference begins to become apparent as we read the last two stanzas, which are mainly a roll call of the missing. The Robinsonian departure is in the way in which these dead are characterized. What, for example, are we to make of the reference to "Clavering / Who died because he couldn't laugh?" Or of "Lingard with his eerie joy"? What of these people, here barely mentioned, but mentioned in connection with tantalizing qualities that are hard to forget, that have in them some of the inexplicably sad individuality that might be—that might as well be—fate? I suspect that one who began as even the most casual reader might wish to know more of these people, and he might then realize that in Robinson's other poems, and only there, he would have a chance of doing so.

A first perusal of "Calverly's" might also lead the perceptive reader to suspect that the poet is more interested in the human personality than he is in, say, nature; that he is interested in people not only for their enigmatic and haunting qualities but also for their mysterious exemplification of some larger entity, some agency that, though it determines both their lives and their deaths, may or may not have any concern for them or knowledge of them. Of these men, the poet cannot say "where their light lives are gone," and because he cannot say—and because there is nothing or no way to tell him—he cannot know, either, what his own fate is, or its meaning; he can know only that he himself was once at Calverly's, that the others who were there are gone, and that he shall follow them in due time. He cannot say what this means or whether, in fact, it means anything. Though he can guess as to what it might mean, all he finally *knows* is what has happened.

This condition of mind is a constant throughout all but a very few of Robinson's poems. It links him in certain curious ways with the existentialists, but we are aware of such affinities only tangentially, for Robinson's writings, whatever else they may be, are dramas that make use of conjecture rather than overt statements of ideas held and defended. It is the fact that truth is "so strange in its nakedness" that appalled and intrigued him—the fact that it takes different forms for different people and different situations. Robinson believed in the unknowable constants that govern the human being from within; in addition, he had the sort of mind that sees history as a unity in which these human constants appear in dramatic form. This explains why he had no difficulty at all in projecting Welsh kingdoms and biblical encounters out of houses and situations he had known in New England, much as his own Shakespeare was able to fill "Ilion, Rome, or any town you like / Of olden time with timeless Englishmen."

The unity of the poet's mind is a quality that is certain to make its presence felt very early in the reader's acquaintance with Robinson. One can tell a great deal about him from the reading of a single poem. All the poems partake of a single view and a single personality, and one has no trouble in associating the poems in strict forms with the more irregular ones as the products of the same vision of existence. The sensibility evidenced by the poems is both devious and tenacious, and it lives most intensely when unresolved about questions dealing with the human personality. Robinson is perhaps the greatest master of the speculative or conjectural approach to the writing of poetry. Uncertainty was the air he breathed, and speculation was not so much a device with him—though at its best it is a surpassingly effective technique—as it was a habit of mind, an integral part of the self. As with most powerful poets, the writing proceeded from the way in which Robinson naturally thought, the way he naturally *was,* and so was inextricably rooted in his reticent, slightly morbid, profoundly contemplative, solitary, compassionate, and stoical personality and was not the product of a conscious search for a literary "way," an unusual manner of speaking which was invented or discovered and in which the will had a major part.

Robinson's tentative point of view was solidly wedded to a style that was exactly the same characteristics as his mind. It makes an artistic virtue, and often a very great one, of arriving at only provisional answers and solutions, of leaving it up to the reader's personality—also fated—to choose from among them the most likely. Thus a salient quality of Robinson's work is the extraordinary roundness and fullness he obtains from such circumlocutions of his subjects, as though he were indeed turning (in William James's phrase) "the cube of reality." One is left with the belief that in any given situation there are many truths—as many, so to speak, as there are persons involved, as there are witnesses, as there are ways of thinking about it. And encompassing all these is the shadowy probability that none of them is or can be final. What we see in Robinson's work is the unending and obsessional effort to make sense of experience when perhaps there is none to be made. The poet, the reader, all of us are members of humanity in the sense Robinson intended when he characterized the earth as "a kind of vast spiritual kindergarten where millions of people are trying to spell God with the wrong blocks."

It is through people that Robinson found the hints and gleams of the universal condition that he could not help trying to solve. Like other human beings, he was cursed with intelligence and sensibility in a universe made for material objects. "The world is a hell of a place," he once said, "but the universe is a fine thing," and again, "We die of what we eat and drink, / But more we die of what we think." Robinson has been perhaps the only American poet—certainly the only one of major status—interested *exclusively* in human beings as subject matter for poetry—in the psychological, motivational aspects of living, in the inner life as it is projected upon the outer. His work is one vast attempt to tell the stories that no man can really tell, for no man can know their real meaning, their real intention, or even whether such exists, though it persistently appears to do so. In all Robinson's people the Cosmos seems to be brooding in one way or another, so that a man and woman sitting in a garden, as in "Mortmain," are, in *what* they are, exemplars of eternal laws that we may guess at but not know. The laws are present in psychological constitutions as surely as they are in physical materials, in the orbital patterns of stars and planets and atoms, only deeper hid, more tragic and mysterious, "as there might somewhere be veiled / Eternal reasons why the tricks of time / Were played like this."

Robinson wrote an enormous amount of poetry (how one's mind quails at the sheer *weight*, the physical bulk, of his fifteen-hundred-page *Collected Poems*!), but at the center of it and all through it is the Personality, the Mind, conditioned by its accidental placement in time and space—these give the individuations that make drama possible—but also partaking of the hidden universals, the not-to-be-knowns that torment all men. In these poems "the strange and unremembered light / That is in dreams" plays over "The nameless and eternal tragedies / That render hope and hopelessness akin." Like a man speaking under torture—or self-torture—Robinson tells of these things, circling them, painfully shifting from one possible interpretation to another, and the reader circles with him, making, for want of any received, definitive opinion, hesitant, troubling, tentative judgments. The result is an unresolved view, but a view of remarkable richness and suggestibility, opening out in many directions and unsealing many avenues of possibility: a multidimensional view that the reader is left pondering as the poem has pondered, newly aware of his own enigmas, of what he and his own life—its incidents and fatalities—may mean, could mean, and thus he is likely to feel himself linked into the insoluble universal equation, in which nature itself is only a frame of mind, a projection of inwardness, tormenting irresolution, and occasional inexplicable calms.

> she could look
> Right forward through the years, nor any more
> Shrink with a cringing prescience to behold
> The glitter of dead summer on the grass,
> Or the brown-glimmered crimson of still trees
> Across the intervale where flashed along,
> Black-silvered, the cold river.

II

As has been said, Robinson's method—which on some fronts has been labeled antipoetic—would not amount to as much as it does were not the modes of thought presented in such powerful and disturbing dramatic forms. For an "antipoet," Robinson was an astonishing craftsman. One has only to read a few of his better poems in the classic French repetitive forms, such as "The House on the Hill," to recognize the part that traditional verse patterns play in his work. This much is demonstrable. It is among those who believe the poetic essence to lie somewhere outside or beyond such considerations, somewhere in the image-making, visual, and visionary realm, that Robinson's position has been challenged. And it is true that his verse is oddly bare, that there are few images in it—though, of these, some are very fine indeed—and that most of it is highly cerebral and often written in a scholarly or pseudoscholarly manner that is frequently more than a little pedantic. Many of his poems contain an element of self-parody, and these carry more than their share of bad, flat, stuffy writing.

> There were slaves who dragged the shackles of a precedent
>   unbroken,
> Demonstrating the fulfillment of unalterable schemes,
> Which had been, before the cradle, Time's inexorable tenants
> Of what were now the dusty ruins of their fathers' dreams.

Infrequently there is also a kind of belaboring-beyond-belaboring of the obvious:

> The four square somber things that you see first
> Around you are four walls that go as high
> As to the ceiling.

And now and then one comes on philosophical pronouncements of a remarkable unconvincingness, demonstrating a total failure of idiom, of art:

> Too much of that
> May lead you by and by through gloomy lanes
> To a sad wilderness, where one may grope
> Alone, and always, or until he feels
> Ferocious and invisible animals
> That wait for men and eat them in the dark.

At his worst, Robinson seems to go on writing long after whatever he has had to say about the subject has been exhausted; there is a suspicious look of automatism about his verse instrument. The reader, being made of less stern stuff, will almost always fail before Robinson's blank verse does.

Robinson certainly wrote too much. Like Wordsworth—even more than Wordsworth, if that is possible—he is in need of selective editing. In the present book, this is what the late Morton Dauwen Zabel has done, and I believe with singular success. The Robinson of this book is much more nearly the essential, the permanently valuable Robinson than the Robinson of the *Collected Poems,* though there are unavoidable exclusions—particularly of the good book-length poems, such as *Lancelot* and *Merlin*—which one might legitimately regret and to which it is hoped that the reader will eventually have recourse. Yet even in the present volume one is likely to be put off by the length of many of the pieces. Then, too, if the casual reader skims only a little of a particular poem and finds that nothing much is happening or that event, action, and resolution are taking place only in various persons' minds, he is also likely to shy away. But once *in* the poem, committed to it, with his mind winding among the alternative complexities of Robinson's characters' minds—that is, winding with Robinson's mind— the reader changes slowly, for Robinson hath his will. One is held by the curious dry magic that seems so eminently unmagical, that bears no resemblance to the elfin or purely verbal or native-woodnote magic for which English verse is justly celebrated. It is a magic for which there is very little precedent in all literature. Though external affinities may be asserted and even partially demonstrated with Praed and Browning, though there are occasional distant echoes of Wordsworth, Keats, Hardy, and Rossetti, Robinson is really like none of them in his root qualities; his spell is cast with none of the traditional paraphernalia, but largely through his own reading of character and situation and fate, his adaptation of traditional poetic devices to serve these needs—an adaptation so unexpected, so revolutionary, as to seem not so much adaptation as transformation.

Another odd thing about Robinson is that his best work and his worst are yet remarkably alike. The qualities that make the good poems good are the same qualities that make the bad poems bad; it is only a question of how Robinson's method works out in, "takes to," the situation he is depicting, and often the difference between good, bad, and mediocre is thin indeed. This difficulty is also compounded by the fact that Robinson is equally skilled as a technician in both memorable poems and trivial ones. In the less interesting poems, particularly the longer ones, Robinson's air of portentousness can be tiresome. Reading these, one is tempted to say that Robinson is the most prolific *reticent* poet in history. Though he gives the impression that he is reluctant to write down what he is writing, he often goes on and on, in a kind of intelligent mumbling, a poetical wringing of the hands, until the reader becomes restive and a little irritated. In these passages, Robinson's verse instrument has a certain kinship with the salt maker in the fairy tale, grinding away of its own accord at the bottom of the sea. Then there is the gray, austere landscape of the poems, the lack of background definition. One is accustomed to finding the characters in a poem—particularly a narrative poem—in a *place,* a location with objects and a weather of its own, a world which the reader can enter and in which he can, as it were, live with the characters. But there is very little of the environmental in Robinson's work. What few gestures and concessions he makes to the outside world are token ones; all externality is quickly devoured by the tormented introversion of his personages. In Robinson, the mind eats everything and converts it to part of a conflict with self; one could say with some justification that all Robinson's poems are about people who are unable to endure themselves or to resolve their thoughts into some meaningful, cleansing action. So much introversion is not only harrowing; it can also be boring, particularly when carried on to the enormous lengths in which it appears in *Matthias at the Door* and *Avon's Harvest.*

And yet with these strictures, the case against Robinson's poetry has pretty much been stated, and we have on our hands what remains after they have been acknowledged.

III

No poet ever understood loneliness or separateness better than Robinson or knew the self-consuming furnace that the brain can become in isolation, the suicidal hellishness of it, doomed as it is to feed on itself in answerless frustration, fated to this condition by the accident of human birth, which carries with it the hunger for certainty and the intolerable load of personal recollections. He understood loneliness in all its many forms and depths and was thus less interested in its conventional poetic aspects than he was in the loneliness of the man in the crowd, or alone with his thoughts of the dead, or feeling at some unforeseen time the metaphysical loneliness, the *angst,* of being "lost among the stars," or becoming aware of the solitude that resides in comfort and in the affection of friend and family—that desperation at the heart of what is called happiness. It is only the poet and those involved who realize the inevitability and the despair of these situations, "Although, to the serene outsider, / There still would seem to be a way."

The acceptance of the fact that there is no way, that there is nothing to do about the sadness of most human beings when they are alone or speaking to others as if to themselves, that there is nothing to offer them but recognition, sympathy, compassion, deepens Robinson's best poems until we sense in them something other than art. A thing inside us is likely to shift from where it was, and our world view to change, though perhaps only slightly, toward a darker, deeper perspective. Robinson has been called a laureate of failure and has even been accused (if that is the word) of making a cult and a virtue of failure, but that assessment is not quite accurate. His subject was "the slow tragedy of haunted men," those whose "eyes are lit with a wrong light," those who believe that some earthly occurrence in the past (and now forever impossible) could have made all the difference, that some person dead or otherwise beyond reach, some life unlived and now unlivable, could have been the answer to everything. But these longings were seen by Robinson to be the delusions necessary to sustain life, for human beings, though they can live without hope, cannot live believing that no hope ever could have existed. For this reason, many of the poems deal with the unlived life, the man kept by his own nature or by circumstance from "what might have been his," but there is always the ironic Robinsonian overtone that what might have been would not have been much better than what is—and, indeed, might well have been worse; the failure would only have had its development and setting altered somewhat, but not its pain or its inevitability.

Though Robinson's dramatic sense was powerful and often profound, his narrative sense was not. His narrative devices are few, and they are used again and again. The poet is always, for example, running into somebody in the street whom he knew under other circumstances and who is now a bum, a "slowly-freezing Santa Claus," a street-corner revivalist, or something equally comical-pathetic and cut off. The story of the person's passing from his former state to this one then becomes the poem, sometimes told by the derelict, the "ruin who meant well," and sometimes puzzled out by the poet himself, either with his deep, painful probing or, as in some of the later long poems, such as *The Man Who Died Twice*, with an intolerable amount of poetical hemming and hawing, backing and filling.

And yet Robinson's peculiar elliptical vision, even when it is boring, is worth the reader's time. The tone of his voice is so distinctive, his technique so varied and resourceful, and his compassion so intense that something valuable comes through even the most wasteful of his productions. Not nearly enough has been made of Robinson's skill, the chief thing about which is that it is able to create, through an astonishing number of forms and subjects, the tone of a single voice, achieving variety within a tonal unity. And it is largely in this tone, the product of outlook (or, if I may be forgiven, inlook), technique, and personality, that Robinson's particular excellence lies; thus the tone is worth examining.

Robinson's mind was not sensuously rich, if by that is meant a Keatsian

or Hopkinsian outgoingness into nature as a bodily experience and the trust
and delight in nature that this attitude implies. His poetic interests are psychological and philosophical; he examines the splits between what is and
what might have been, what must be and what cannot be. That Robinson
sees these differences to matter very little, finally, does not mean that they
do not matter to the people who suffer from them; it is, in fact, in this realm
of delusionary and obsessive suffering that Robinson's poems take place.
Though his mind was not rich in a sensuous way, it was both powerful and
hesitant, as though suspended between strong magnets. This gives his work
an unparalleled sensitivity in balance; and from this balance, this desperately poised uncertainty, emanates a compassion both very personal and
cosmic—a compassion that one might well see as a substitute for the compassion that God failed to supply. It is ironic at times, it is bitter and self-
mocking, but it is always compassion unalloyed by sentimentality; it has
been earned, as it is the burden of the poems themselves to show. This attitude, this tone, runs from gentle, rueful humor—though based, even so, on
stark constants of human fate such as the aging process and death—to the
most terrible hopelessness. It may appear in the tortuous working out of a
long passage, or it may gleam forth for an instant in surroundings not seen
until its appearance to be frightening, as in the poem below.

"Isaac and Archibald" is a New England pastoral in which a twelve-
year-old boy takes a long walk with an old man, Isaac, to visit another old
man at his farm. Nothing much happens, except that Isaac and Archibald manage to reveal to the boy the signs of mental decline and approaching death in each other. The two men drink cider; the boy sits and reflects,
prefiguring as he does the mature man and poet he will become. The boy's
awareness of death is built up by small, affectionate touches, some of them
so swift and light that they are almost sure to be passed over by the hurried
reader.

> Hardly had we turned in from the main road
> When Archibald, with one hand on his back
> And the other clutching his huge-headed cane,
> Came limping down to meet us.—"Well! well! well!"
> Said he; and then he looked at my red face,
> All streaked with dust and sweat, and shook my hand,
> And said it must have been a right smart walk
> That we had had that day from Tilbury Town.—
> "Magnificent," said Isaac; and he told
> About the beautiful west wind there was

Which cooled and clarified the atmosphere.
"You must have made it with your legs, I guess,"
Said Archibald; and Isaac humored him
With one of those infrequent smiles of his
Which he kept in reserve, apparently,
For Archibald alone. "But why," said he,
"Should Providence have cider in the world
If not for such an afternoon as this?"
And Archibald, with a soft light in his eyes,
Replied that if he chose to go down cellar,
There he would find eight barrels—one of which
Was newly tapped, he said, and to his taste
An honor to the fruit, Isaac approved
Most heartily of that, and guided us
Forthwith, as if his venerable feet
Were measuring the turf in his own door-yard,
Straight to the open rollway. Down we went,
Out of the fiery sunshine to the gloom,
Grateful and half sepulchral, where we found
The barrels, like eight potent sentinels,
Close ranged along the wall. From one of them
A bright pine spile stuck out alluringly,
And on the black flat stone, just under it,
Glimmered a late-spilled proof that Archibald
Had spoken from unfeigned experience.
There was a fluted antique water-glass
Close by, and in it, prisoned, or at rest,
There was a cricket, of the soft brown sort
That feeds on darkness. Isaac turned him out,
And touched him with his thumb to make him jump.

Until the introduction of the cricket and the few words that typify it, there is nothing startling in the passage, though it is quite good Robinson, with the judicious adverb "alluringly" attached to the protrusion of the pine spile and the lovely affectionate irony of Archibald's "unfeigned experience" with the cider. But the cricket, of the *sort* that feeds on darkness, changes the poem and brings it into the central Robinsonian orbit. Here, the insect is a more terrifying and mysterious creature—a better symbol for the context—than a maggot or dead louse would be, for it is normally a benign spirit of household and hearth. This simple way of referring to it, as though the supposition that it "feeds on darkness" were the most obvious and natural thing in the world to say about it, produces a haunting effect when encountered along with the gentle old farmers' proximity to death and the boy's budding awareness of it.

It may be inferred from the above passages that Robinson is not a writer of unremitting brilliance or a master of the more obvious technical virtuosities. He is, rather, as has been said, a poet of quick, tangential thrusts, of sallies and withdrawals, of fleeting hints and glimpsed implications. In his longer poems, particularly, the impacts build up slowly, and it is only to those who have not the sensitivity to catch the sudden, baffling, half-revealing gleams—those who are "annoyed by no such evil whim / As death, or time, or truth"—that Robinson's poems are heavy and dull. Though he has a way, particularly in the later poems, of burying his glints of meaning pretty deeply in the material that makes them possible, Robinson at his best manages to use the massiveness of discourse and the swift, elusive gleam of illumination—the momentary flashing into the open of a stark, tragic hint, a fleeting generalization—as complementaries. And when the balance between these elements is right, the effect is unforgettable.

At times it appears that Robinson not only did not seek to avoid dullness but courted it and actually used it as a device, setting up his major points by means of it and making them doubly effective by contrast, without in the least violating the unity of tone or the huge, heavy drift of the poem toward its conclusion. He is a slow and patient poet; taking his time to say a thing as he wishes to say it is one of his fundamental qualities. This has worked against him, particularly since his work has survived into an age of anything but slow and patient readers. The pedestrian movement of much of his work has made him unpopular in an era when the piling on of startling effects, the cramming of the poetic line with all the spoils it can carry, is regarded not so much as a criterion of good or superior verse of a certain kind, but as poetry itself, other kinds being relegated to inferior categories yet to be defined. But Robinson's considered, unhurried lines, as uncomplicated in syntax as they are difficult in thought, in reality are, by virtue of their enormous sincerity, conviction, and quiet originality, a constant rebuke to those who conceive of poetry as verbal legerdemain or as the "superior amusement" that the late T. S. Eliot would have had it be.

The Robinson line is simple in the way that straightforward English prose is simple; the declarative sentence is made to do most of the work. His questions, though comparatively rare, are weighted with the agony of concern, involvement, and uncertainty. It is the thought, rather than the expression of the thought, that makes some of Robinson difficult, for he was almost always at pains to write simply, and his skills were everywhere subservient to this ideal. My personal favorite of Robinson's effects is his extremely subtle use of the line as a means of changing the meaning of the sentence that forms the line, the whole poem changing direction slightly but unmistakably with each such shift.

> What is it in me that you like so much,
> And love so little?

And yet for all his skill, Robinson's technical equipment is never obvious or obtrusive, as Hopkins's, say, is. This is, of course, a tribute to his resourcefulness, for in his best pieces the manner of the poem is absorbed into its matter, and we focus not on the mode of saying but on the situations and characters into whose presence we have come.

IV

Robinson's favorite words, because they embody his favorite way of getting at any subject, are "may" and "might." The whole of the once-celebrated "The Man against the Sky," for example, is built upon their use. When the poet sees a man climbing Mount Monadnock, it is, for the purposes of his poem, important that he *not* know who the man is or what he is doing there, so that the poem can string together a long series of conjectural possibilities as to who he might be, what might happen to him, and what he might conceivably represent.

> Even he, who stood where I had found him,
> On high with fire all around him,
> Who moved along the molten west,
> And over the round hill's crest
> That seemed half ready with him to go down,
> Flame-bitten and flame-cleft,
> As if there were to be no last thing left
> Of a nameless unimaginable town—
> Even he who climbed and vanished may have taken
> Down to the perils of a depth not known.

When he reaches the words "may have," the reader is in true Robinson country; he lives among alternatives, possibilities, doubts, and delusionary gleams of hope. This particular poem, which not only uses this approach but virtually hounds it to death, is not successful mainly because Robinson insists on being overtly philosophical and, at the end, on committing him-

self to a final view. Another shortcoming is that he is not sufficiently close
to the man, for his poems are much better when he knows *something* of the
circumstances of a human life, tells what he knows, and *then* speculates, for
the unresolved quality of his ratiocinations, coupled with the usually terrible *facts,* enables him to make powerful and haunting use of conjecture
and of his typical "may have" or "might not have" presentations of alternative possibilities.

It is also true of this poem that it has very little of the leavening of
Robinson's irony, and this lack is detrimental to it. This irony has been
widely commented upon, but not, I think, quite as accurately as it might
have been. Though it infrequently has the appearance of callousness or even
cruelty, a closer examination, a more receptive *feeling* of its effect, will usually show that it is neither. It is, rather, a product of a detachment based on
helplessness, on the saving grace of humor that is called into play because
nothing practical can be done and because the spectator of tragedy must
find some way in which to save himself emotionally from the effects of what
he has witnessed.

> No, no—forget your Cricket and your Ant,
> For I shall never set my name to theirs
> That now bespeak the very sons and heirs
> Incarnate of Queen Gossip and King Cant.
> The case of Leffingwell is mixed, I grant,
> And futile seems the burden that he bears;
> But are we sounding his forlorn affairs
> Who brand him parasite and sycophant?
>
> I tell you, Leffingwell was more than these;
> And if he prove a rather sorry knight,
> What quiverings in the distance of what light
> May not have lured him with high promises,
> And then gone down?—He may have been deceived;
> He may have lied—he did; and he believed.

The irony here is not based on showing in what ridiculous and humil-
iating ways the self-delusion of Leffingwell made of him a parasite and sy-
cophant; it works through and past these things to the much larger propo-
sition that such delusion is necessary to life; that, in fact, it is the condition
that enables us to function at all. The manufacture and protection of the
self-image is really the one constant, the one obsessive concern, of our ex-

istence. This idea was, of course, not new with Robinson, though it may be worth mentioning that many psychiatrists, among them Alfred Adler and Harry Stack Sullivan, place a primary emphasis on such interpretations of the human mentality. What should be noted is that the lies of Leffingwell and of Uncle Ananias are in their way truths, for they have in them that portion of the truth that comes not from fact but from the ideal.

> All summer long we loved him for the same
> Perennial inspiration of his lies.

There is something more here, something more positive, than there is in the gloomy and one-dimensional use of similar themes in, say, Eugene O'Neill's *The Iceman Cometh,* for in Robinson's poems the necessity to lie (and, with luck, sublimely) is connected to the desire to remake the world by remaking that portion of it that is oneself. Robinson shows the relation between such lies and the realities they must struggle to stay alive among, and he shows them with the shrewdness and humor of a man who has told such lies to himself but sadly knows them for what they are. The reader is likely to smile at the absurdity—but also to be left with a new kind of admiration for certain human traits that he had theretofore believed pathetic or contemptible.

V

These, then, are Robinson's kinds of originality, of poetic value—all of them subtle and half-hidden, muffled and disturbing, answering little but asking those questions that are unpardonable, unforgettable, and necessary.

It is curious and wonderful that this scholarly, intelligent, childlike, tormented New England stoic, "always hungry for the nameless," always putting in the reader's mouth "some word that hurts your tongue," unless for anything but his art, protected by hardier friends all his life, but enormously courageous and utterly dedicated (he once told Chard Powers Smith at the very end of his life, "I could never have done *anything* but write poetry"), should have brought off what in its quiet, searching, laborious way is one of the most remarkable accomplishments of modern poetry. Far from indulging, as his detractors have maintained, in a kind of poetical know-nothingism, he actually brought to poetry a new kind of approach, making of a refusal to pronounce definitively on his subjects a virtue and of speculation upon possibilities an instrument that allows an unparalleled fullness to his presentations, as well as endowing them with some of the mysteriousness, futility, and proneness to multiple interpretation that incidents and lives possess in the actual world.

Robinson's best poetry is exactly that kind of communication that "tells the more the more it is not told." In creating a body of major poetry with devices usually thought to be unfruitful for the creative act—irresolution, abstraction, conjecture, a dry, nearly imageless mode of address that tends always toward the general without ever supplying the resolving judgment that we expect of generalization—Robinson has done what good poets have always done: by means of his "cumulative silences" as well as by his actual lines, he has forced us to reexamine and finally to redefine what poetry is—or our notion of it—and so has enabled poetry itself to include more, to *be* more, than it was before he wrote.

HYATT H. WAGGONER

The Idealist in Extremis

Miniver Cheevy, child of scorn,
    Grew lean while he assailed the seasons;
  He wept that he was ever born,
    And he had reasons.
            —ROBINSON, "Miniver Cheevy"

Robinson is perhaps the greatest master of the speculative or conjectural approach to the writing of poetry.
            —JAMES DICKEY, Introduction to
                Selected Poems of E. A. R.

When Emily Dickinson died in 1886, Robinson was in high school in Gardiner, Maine, already experimenting with verse forms. Ten years later, he published his first volume. The two poets were separated in time by only thirty-nine years, a long generation, and in space by the distance between Amherst and Gardiner, which even under the travel conditions of that day was not very great. Yet reading their verse, one might suppose that the two had been born aeons and worlds apart, so much that was vital to both of them had happened in the thirty-nine years between their birth dates.

Dickinson had grown up at a time when even in a college town in the Connecticut valley, Christianity, in the form of late Calvinist dogmatics, had seemed powerful enough to challenge, and Mr. Emerson of Boston and Concord just the man to challenge it. Robinson grew up at a time when even in a small town in Maine, if the town had an educated professional class, as Gardiner had, Christianity in any of its historic forms was coming

From *American Poets: From the Puritans to the Present.* © 1968, 1984 by Hyatt H. Waggoner. Louisiana State University Press, 1984.

to seem unworthy of the attention of thinking people, and Emerson, though greatly honored as a sage, seemed not to be addressing himself to current problems. So far as he was an active influence now, it was chiefly through Mary Baker Eddy, who had found in his Idealism the inspiration for her system of Christian Science, which was spreading rapidly though without touching the most highly educated. To them it was apparent that any religious belief at all, including Emerson's, had been revealed as wishful thinking by the facts uncovered by science. In what the new president of Cornell University called the "History of the Warfare of Science with Theology in Christendom," science had definitely won what appeared to be a final victory; and in the less heralded warfare of science with transcendentalism, victory seemed almost as certain. When nature was viewed in "the light of day," mystic intuitions had a way of evaporating even for John Burroughs, who loved nature as much as any man could.

Scientific naturalism in the 1890s—a philosophy already so remote from us today that we must exercise all our powers of historical imagination to recreate it—had no room in its strictly defined view of reality for anything miraculous, whether "the miraculous" meant biblical miracles or Emerson's "natural supernaturalism," his strategy of making God chiefly immanent. It had no room for intuition either, or for nature as symbolic revelation, or for Emerson's idea of the self as transcendent of time and place. The new philosophy conceived both man and nature on the model of machines. Anything transcendental must be either unreal or completely unknowable—which would perhaps amount to the same thing.

Robinson's name for this new philosophy was simply "materialism." By that word he meant to include both what is sometimes called "mechanism," the idea that reality, human and nonhuman alike, is best compared to a machine, which has neither freedom nor spontaneity; and also what is called, in a more limited sense than his, "materialism," which is the view that reality, all that is, consists exclusively of what can be weighed and measured. From this point of view, anything that cannot be stated in quantitative terms and reduced to law is unreal. Clearly, this point of view made Emerson seem no less naive than Luther or Calvin or St. Paul—perhaps more so indeed.

It was the British Darwinian Herbert Spencer, who is taken seriously by no present-day philosopher I know of, who first broke the bad news to Robinson that what the science of the time could deal with was all there *was* to be dealt with. Like Hamlin Garland and Theodore Dreiser and many other Americans of the period, Robinson felt that however unpleasant the new doctrine might be, simple honesty, respect for *facts,* required that he accept it. If it seemed to render life meaningless by denying reality to everything qualitative, including all the values by which man had always thought his life could acquire meaning, perhaps we should acknowledge that life *is* meaningless. "Life was something before you came to Spencer," Robinson wrote a friend in 1890. But two years later, while a special student at Harvard from 1891 to 1893, he found himself reading some Emerson, during a mastoid attack, "in order to drive the pain away." Not surprisingly, in view of the position from which he approached them, he felt that he got very little out of the essays on "Friendship" and "Love."

From Josiah Royce's expounding of Absolute Idealism he got even less, indeed "absolutely nothing," he once wrote a friend. He took to writing letters in class while the irrelevant lectures went on. But toward William James he found himself unable to maintain his lofty indifference. James challenged him harder and evoked a fine scorn of both the man and his ideas. Precisely what it was about James's ideas that Robinson didn't like, his letters do not make clear, except in one respect: James's thinking was incompatible with Spencerian monistic naturalism.

Robinson decided that the reason this "metaphysical funny man" with his "spiritual vulgarity" talked the way he did was that he had either not read, or had not understood, Spencer. In 1898, five years after he had left Harvard as a student, he was still expressing his fierce contempt for James. Years later, at the MacDowell Colony, he surprised a friend and fellow colonist by coming in to breakfast one day and without any warning, or any relevance to anything that had been said, launching into a vehement denunciation and clever parody of James and several others among his Harvard professors as "stuffed shirts" and pretenders who had had nothing to teach him. This outburst was so unlike Robinson, who was generally so quiet, retiring, and kindly in his judgments, that the friend remembered the incident vividly. We can only suppose that Robinson must have spent one of many sleepless nights brooding on the matter, to have had to get it off his chest at breakfast this way.

Throughout the 1890s Robinson wavered between the fierce loyalty to Spencer that made him reject Royce and James, and an increasingly warm response to Emerson, to whom he returned in the middle of the decade, after his mother's death, under the influence of a Christian Science friend. Beset by grief and loss—his father, his mother, and his older brother Dean all died in the 1890s—and often ill himself, he desperately sought consolation wherever he might find it. He went back to Carlyle, whom he had read before going to college, and decided now that *Sartor Resartus* and Christianity, Jesus and "illuminated commonsense," all pointed in the same direction, toward "a denial of the existence of matter as anything but a manifestation of thought." Shortly after his mother's death in 1896 he announced that he was "very glad to be able to stand up and say that I am an idealist. Perhaps idealism is the philosophy of desperation, but I do not think so." Rereading St. John's Gospel in the light of his new idealism, he found it making sense to him for the first time.

During a period of trouble with his eyes, he had a friend read to him.

> J. and I are reading up (J. is reading and I am listening) on Oriental Religions. I have been interested to find out that Christianity is in reality nothing more than Buddhism humanized; and that Nirvana and Heaven are from the idealist's point of view—which is to me the only point of view—pretty much the same thing. . . .
>
> I have just read Emerson on "The Oversoul." If you do not know it, for heaven's sake get hold of it.

His "conversion" to a really firm faith in what he took to be the core of meaning common to the teachings of Jesus, Buddhism, Carlyle, and Emerson was short-lived, but for a while it seemed to him to make him better able to endure life's torture chamber. "How long do you think a man can live in hell?" he asked a friend in 1897. No one, he thought, could be happy in such an age as his, when "the whole trend of popular thought" was "in the wrong direction." But he was strong enough now, perhaps, he thought, with the help of his new philosophy, to get along without happiness, to endure the results of having been born at the wrong time. Now that he was assured that light *could* be found by those not self-blinded, he could afford to joke at times about an age that was proud of its materialism:

> The age is all right, material progress is all right, Herbert Spencer is all right, hell is all right. These things are temporal necessities, but they are damned uninteresting to one who can get a glimpse of the real light through the clouds of time.

But hell was not always so easy to dismiss. When the glimpses of the light were slow in coming, Robinson more and more found his best help in Emerson.

Returning to him again and again all through the 1890s, he kept finding new depths of meaning he had formerly missed. When he came to *The Conduct of Life* in 1899, he confessed to a friend "with burning shame" that this was a *first* reading. He decided that he liked this late Emerson better than the Emerson of the essays: Here there was more "humanity and humor," less contrast with his own "diabolical system." This was the book, he now realized, that one ought to start with. It revived his faith in Emerson's wisdom. But as time went on and the first effects of his conversion wore off, he began to value the poetry more and the prose less, until at last, late in life, he could say to a friend at the MacDowell Colony:

> Emerson wrote some of the purest poetry we have in America—though not a great deal of it. The trouble is, nobody reads it. And most people don't know it exists. They get side-tracked to "Self-Reliance" or "The Oversoul."

But it was not as a "pure" poet that Emerson had first attracted Robinson, or even as a poet at all, but as a consoler and strengthener. In Robinson's later public comments on Emerson, we may find something of the same innocent covering of tracks that may be seen in *The Torrent and the Night Before* and *The Children of the Night*. Emerson's influence is apparent in both books, particularly—much more than has been realized—in the later one, but Emerson's name never appears in either one. There are poetic tributes to Zola, Crabbe, Thomas Hood, Hardy, Calderon, Verlaine, and Whitman, but none to Emerson. Why not?

When these books came out in 1896 and 1897, Robinson had not yet begun to respond to Emerson as a writer like himself to whom one might pay literary tribute. Emerson was the "sage" who had been of incalculable help to him in time of trouble, not an artist from whom one might learn something about how to write. Despite the later high praise of Emerson as poet, it is doubtful that Robinson ever did learn anything about the poet's craft from him, more's the pity. At any rate it is very clear that Emerson the priest and prophet was not, in the 1890s, a part of Robinson's "literary" experience at all, but his chief secret spiritual resource.

Increasingly, Robinson found it embarrassing to acknowledge publicly this particular source of consolation. It must have come to him fairly early—I should guess by 1902, the date of *Captain Craig*, though I have found no evidence in the letters to substantiate this guess—it must have occurred to him that if William James were vulnerable to the charge that his thought ignored Spencer's naturalism, Emerson's philosophy was even more vulnerable. All his life Robinson continued to read books of popular science and scientific philosophy, and the trends he observed therein, though he might think them "all wrong," yet left him more and more on the defensive. Those with better minds than his, he observed, were all, or so it seemed to him, becoming mechanistic naturalists. His early Harvard and Gardiner friend, Lawrence J. Henderson, teaching biological chemistry at Harvard, was not alone in reducing life to "nothing but" a physiochemical mechanism. This was what science seemed to have discovered by its rigorous methods of truth-seeking. How was a mere poet, who could claim neither mystic revelation nor competence in philosophy, to answer? Surely not by saying, "But I have read Emerson, and he intuited divinity everywhere."

So far as I have been able to discover, it was not until 1916, when he was nearly fifty, that Robinson could bring himself to pay any sort of *public* tribute to Emerson. In that year he told Joyce Kilmer in an interview that he considered Emerson our greatest American poet, and thought that his best things, fragments usually rather than whole poems, were as great as anything ever written anywhere in any language. His praise thus exceeded even that of Frost, who would later call "Uriel" the "greatest *Western*"— that is, American—"poem yet."

It is not surprising that this tribute of one poet to another says nothing about Emerson's usefulness to Robinson in his struggle with materialism, even though Robinson would soon publish "The Man against the Sky," the whole point of which was to reject materialism. But that he had not completely reversed himself on Emerson, and would indeed never really do so, is suggested not only by his last poems, but, more explicitly, by one of his last letters. Writing from the hospital bed where he was dying of cancer to a young correspondent who was in difficulty, he repeated Dickinson's gesture of sharing a source of her own strength with Mrs. Higginson by sending her a volume of Emerson. "Perhaps Emerson will help," he wrote his young correspondent.

Emerson's influence on the poetry increases perceptibly through Robinson's first three volumes, then drops off after *Captain Craig*, finally to return to prominence in the last two long poems. If the preceding account, drawn from letters and other sources of information external to the poetry, is sound, this is what we should expect to find, providing just one more piece of external evidence is added.

Late in his life Robinson was much cheered by the new climate of scientific philosophy that began to be apparent in some quarters in the middle and later 1920s. Reading the British astrophysicists Eddington and Jeans, who were Platonists and religious in tone, Robinson was encouraged to hope once more that his implicit transcendentalism would not in the end prove utterly indefensible. There was, he decided in 1933, a new "nontheological" religion on the way, to be "revealed" by science when we had the wits to see it. To an age when churches were only buildings and theology had lost all meaning, the coming religion would bring fresh hope and a renewed faith in the transcendent self. This new confidence of Robinson's lies behind the affirmations he intended to make in *Amaranth* and *King Jasper.*

But to return to the beginning of the career. Emerson's presence is not very obvious in *The Torrent and the Night Before,* or very important, but it is perceptible in at least four of the poems, and perhaps in others. What chiefly dominates the book, of course, is the sense of loss and grief, but Emerson provides a contrapuntal theme. To begin where one might not expect to find him, the sonnet in praise of Zola shows Robinson thinking in Emersonian terms about a naturalist of whom he knew little. He had read, he later confessed, only one book by Zola before writing the poem, and he had apparently not grasped the philosophic intention of *that* one. If Zola had been able to read the sonnet, he would no doubt have wondered whether the author's use of his name as the title were not a mistake; for in the poem he is praised not for anything he had said in *The Experimental Novel* he wanted to accomplish, but rather for penetrating through appearances to "the human heart / Of God" and thus helping us all to find and cherish "the divine heart of man"—two hearts being really, it is implied, the same heart. The doctrine assumed here is very good Emersonianism but very bad naturalism of the Zola variety.

There is a good deal in "The Children of the Night" that is straight out of Emerson, which may be one of the reasons why the poem was later omitted from the *Collected Poems.* Such Emersonian counsels as

> So let us in ourselves revere
> The Self which is the Universe!

sound like Robinson only in the smoothness of their meter. "Credo," which tells us more about what Robinson would like to believe, or hopes some day to believe, than about anything he actually does believe, almost certainly gets the suggestions for its images of music and light and darkness from Emerson's "The Poet"—the poem, not the essay—as these pairs of lines partially suggest:

> I see the coming light,
> I see the scattered gleams,
> Aloft, beneath, on left and right
> The stars' own ether beams.
> ("The Poet")

> I cannot find my way: there is no star
> In all the shrouded heavens anywhere;
> . . . .
> I know the far-sent message of the years,
> I feel the coming glory of the Light!
>
> ("Credo")

The important substitutions in Robinson's poem are in the verbs: In place of Emerson's concrete and positive "I *see* . . . I *see* . . . ether *beams*," we have the negatives of Robinson's first two lines (he does *not* see, there *is no* star), followed by affirmatives entirely different from Emerson's, affirmatives that have little to say about *present experience*. For the "know" is equivalent to "know about" or "have heard about" the message from the past; and the light in the last line is still not *seen*, not experienced directly, only "felt," and even so not felt as *light* but felt as "glory." So that in effect this poem whose title says "I believe" contains neither belief nor experience from which belief might proceed, but only memory and hope. The poem suggests the predicament of an Emerson born too late, into a wrong world, as a child of the night who cannot honestly and simply assert, "I see."

But "Two Sonnets" makes Emerson's relation to this early poetry of Robinson's still clearer. The two poems are meant to be read together, and together they take off from a line in "Monadnoc," one of Emerson's greatest poems and one of Robinson's favorites, even this early, no doubt partly because the concluding lines of the poem affirm, in a manner more rare in Emerson's poetry than in his prose, his belief in the permanence of individual life. The mountain, Emerson writes, shames us at times, and humbles us always, but also, for those capable of seeing its meanings, enlarges and purifies our faith:

> Mute orator! well skilled to plead,
> And send conviction without phrase,
> Thou dost succor and remede
> The shortness of our days,
> And promise, on thy Founder's truth,
> Long morrow to this mortal youth.

While still searching for a way to accommodate himself to his mother's death, in the interval between the publication of his first volume in 1896 and his second in 1897, Robinson, writing a friend about his grief, misquoted, without identifying them, two earlier lines from Emerson's poem:

"For the world was made in order, and the atoms march in time," he wrote. Emerson had written

> For the world was built in order,
> And the atoms march in tune,

by his last word suggesting the *melodiousness* of reality, an image which the immediately following lines take up and extend.

The first of Robinson's "Two Sonnets" comments on the conclusion of "Monadnoc," saying, in effect, yes, man *is* immortal, but immortality carries with it no memory of our earthly existence. We must not, the sonnet concludes, "cherish, in the life that is to come, / The scattered features of dead friends again." The poem never says, but its tone suggests, that the reason is that life is too painful to be remembered.

The second sonnet is a comment on the earlier lines that Robinson misquoted in his letter. Just as the first one had said "Yes, *but*" to Emerson's belief that nature's revelations had as their ultimate implication man's immortality, so this sonnet too says "Yes, *but*" to Emerson's vision of cosmic harmony. Robinson accepts the vision but devotes his poem to stating the *difficulty* of attaining it. It is perhaps, he thinks, too demanding a vision for most of us. "Never until our souls are strong enough," the sonnet begins, "To plunge into the crater of the Scheme," not until we are morally and intellectually reborn somehow, "are we to get / Where atoms and the ages are one stuff." We shall not be able to know how "the cursed waste / Of life"—his mother's early death, for instance—is consistent with "the beneficence divine" that manifests itself in starlight and sunlight and "soul-shine"—not, that is, "Till we have drunk . . . The mead of Thought's prophetic endlessness."

The two sonnets are not likely to strike most of us today as very good poems, partly because their very involved obscurities can hardly be unraveled unless we have Emerson's "Monadnoc" in mind, but unravel all too easily if we do, leaving the poems to be compared with Emerson's much greater one—a comparison wholly to Emerson's benefit. So I shall spend no more time on them, except the time it takes to say that Robinson's translation of Emerson's lines as implying a *place* "where atoms and the ages are one stuff" seems to fit in, in a curious way, with the particular form of his misquotation of the second line, his changing "tune" to "time." At any rate, Robinson's version in the sonnet omits much of both the poetry and the theology of Emerson's concrete and imagistic lines and strikes me as a very cloudy image indeed, if it *is* an image and not rather a vague concept.

As a result of Robinson's intensive, grief-motivated rereading of Emerson in late 1896 and early 1897, his second volume, *The Children of the Night,* is markedly more Emersonian than his first. For the most part, the contents of the two volumes are the same, but two poems in the first volume were dropped in the second, and a number of new ones were added. The longest, and thematically the most important, of the additions was a series of meditative poems called simply "Octaves," twenty-five of them in all. They have a single subject, Robinson's attempt to come to terms with Emerson. They state Robinson's agreement in theory with the one he calls now "the master," and at the same time sometimes merely imply and again explicitly state his inability to feel the way the "master," who is never named, felt: "Truth neither shakes / Nor wavers; but the world shakes, and we shriek."

The speaker in the "Octaves" makes a central theme out of his awareness that he cannot measure up to the standards set by Emerson. He can *admire* the faith of the master, but not really, he fears, *hold* it. The first Octave will have to be a sufficient illustration of this theme which runs throughout the series:

> We thrill too strangely at the master's touch;
> We shrink too sadly from the larger self
> Which for its own completeness agitates
> And undermines us; we do not feel—
> We dare not feel it yet—the splendid shame
> Of uncreated failure; we forget,
> The while we groan, that God's accomplishment
> Is always and unfailingly at hand.

Emersonian terms, or Robinson's equivalents of them, are used throughout what is in effect a twenty-five-part dialogue between the two, but Emerson's *meaning,* as rendered here to be contrasted with the speaker's own difficulty in attaining belief, is never quite the same as what Emerson meant. Throughout the poems we get terms and phrases like "All-Soul," "Truth" considered as "divine, transitional, transcendent," and the "Real" in contrast with the merely actual of "this life"; yet the speaker quite clearly is thinking of the master's system as a defensive *retreat* from a discredited orthodoxy, while Emerson himself thought of transcendentalism as a recovery of original religious insights. Emerson had worked out his point of view, as he saw it, not as a substitute for a faith rendered philosophically obsolete by Darwin and Spencer but in part at least in reaction against the cold and increasingly practical moralism of the Unitarian movement, and in part as a way of mastering his own special and personal impotence and dread. As he saw it, after he had worked out his new ideas, Unitarianism, with its emphasis on reason and morality, was a church without a religion. The vital element in any real religion consisted of direct response to God within, in religious *experience* in short. Pondering what he ought to do with his life now that he was out of the Unitarian ministry, he went to the White Mountains to meditate and read, particularly to read, and read about, George Fox, the Quaker mystic. Fox had lived his life as though he knew that "God IS, not WAS." This, Emerson decided, was the only knowledge that was wholly essential.

This mystical and antinomian core of transcendentalism, the elements that later led Emerson to declare that the movement ought to be described as "a Saturnalia of faith," could never be inferred from anything in Robinson's "Octaves." The "master" is a wise man who knows how important it is to believe in the Soul, and finds fewer obstacles to doing so than the speaker in the poems. Recalling the delight Robinson experienced several years after writing the "Octaves" when he first discovered *The Conduct of Life,* we can see that he was prepared to prefer the late Emerson, the theistic humanist, prepared before he ever read him. This late Emerson, he said, had more "humanity" and "humor": precisely, and less commitment to mystic experience. The late Emerson was something like an oriental sage, but a sage who had given up Zen's concentration on the immediate perception of being in depth. The late Emerson was less confident than he once had been that experience was equivalent to revelation. No wonder Robinson felt greater kinship with him. The wonder is that the Emerson we met in "Octaves" is already old before Robinson had any way of knowing from his reading what Emerson would become. Robinson seems to have arrived at his interpretation by subtracting from transcendentalism the elements that were meaningless to him in terms of his own experience. What was left after all the subtractions was a sort of Stoical idealism.

The two "Octaves" that state the most unequivocal agreement with Emerson were, significantly, omitted from the *Collected Poems.* They are on art, and the role of the poet, and there is nothing at all in them which is not Emersonian—though there is much in Emerson that is not in *them.* For several years Robinson felt that on this subject he had no differences with the master. But as he began to see that metaphysics and aesthetics are not unrelated, I think he became embarrassed by the explicit Emersonianism of these two "Octaves" and so took them out of his works. They remind us of another poem he decided not to include in his collected works, his tribute to Walt Whitman, beginning

> The master-songs are ended, and the man
> That sang them is a name. And so is God
> A name; and so is love, and life, and death,

and continuing to lament the fact that "We do not hear him very much to-day" for "His piercing and eternal cadence rings / Too pure for us." Years later, Robinson said he had "never gotten much" out of Whitman—as we might guess by the extreme generality of the poem that praises him—but why write the tribute, then? It is possible, of course, that the older Robinson simply *forgot* one of his early enthusiasms. But it seems to me much more likely that the late statement was accurate, and that the poetic tribute was written in response neither to Whitman's actual works, nor to the actual man, but to Whitman thought of as a symbol of a secure Emersonian faith. If this is so, the decision not to collect the poem would suggest the waning of Robinson's own faith.

Emerson's impact on Robinson's work is clearest and most pervasive in *Captain Craig,* Robinson's third volume, which appeared five years after *The Children of the Night* and reflected the intensive rereading of Emerson that Robinson was doing in 1899 and 1900. That *this* should be the volume in which Robinson most carefully covered his tracks is one of the things that makes the work interesting to the literary historian.

A single example of careful track-covering will illustrate. Among the poems Robinson added to this volume, in addition to the long title poem, were two that he called, in print, "The Sage" and "Erasmus." But who, we might wonder, is the "sage" referred to? Reading the letters, we need not wonder long. "I am trying to do something with my Emerson and Erasmus sonnets," he wrote a friend in 1900. No sonnet in either *Captain Craig* or the *Collected Poems* is called "Emerson," but the evidence makes it clear that the two poems he was referring to in the letter are the ones called, both in *Captain Craig* and later in *Collected Poems,* "The Sage" and "Erasmus." What he was apparently doing with them was revising them to make them a pair in which each would provide a comment on the other.

In the first of the two as we now have them, the sage is praised for having preserved for us "the mintage of Eternity" by going "back to fierce wisdom and the Orient." The sage himself, "previsioned of the madness and the mean," has found the Truth hidden within "Love's inner shrine" without being "scarred," as the Orient has been, by his contact with "the Unseen." He remains "unfevered and serene" because he was "foreguarded" when he went "back to the perilous gates of Truth."

This seems a curious, and perhaps inept, way to praise Emerson—until

we remember that Robinson is now thinking of the Emerson who wrote
The Conduct of Life, discovered by Robinson while he was working on this
volume. The author of *this* book might well be described as "unfevered and
serene."

The subjects of the two poems have much in common as Robinson
describes them. Both are men of religious vision who came into conflict with
religious authority. The unnamed sage of the first poem is praised for having
gone *"back"* (which is very much emphasized, both the second and the third
lines starting "Back to"), back to an older and fiercer revelation, while Erasmus in the second poem is praised for looking *forward* to the world's need
for more than the medieval "crusts" of divinity. One sage recovers what
had been lost, the other anticipates a need; both were called heretics by the
conservative. The two poems read together seem to imply that both recovery and reform are necessary for the proper guarding of the "mintage of
Eternity."

But why in a pair of poems about two sages is one sage left anonymous
while the other is named? With no direct evidence available of what went
on in Robinson's mind beyond that in the poems themselves, I think it is
still possible to guess. It was too late, in 1900, to be seeming to affirm
Emersonian idealism, even Robinson's guarded late-Emerson variety. If one
should be called upon to stand up and explain what he meant by equating
the power of the Unseen with the rending of the curtain guarding the inner
shrine in Love's temple, what could he possibly say? How explain what
"Eternity" meant to a friend like Henderson? Better not to try, and so better
not to encourage such questions.

The second sonnet of the pair would make it clear whose thought was
being drawn on in both poems even if we did not have the external evidence
identifying the sage as Emerson. The octave of the sonnet describes Erasmus
in such a way as to imply that his humanistic awareness of "the man within
the monk" frightened a Church that had lost touch with both man and God
into charging him with "recreance" and "heresy." The sestet both makes
this implication explicit and reveals that the literary model of a rebel against
religious authority that Robinson *really* has in mind in describing Erasmus
is not, as we might expect if the poem had been written by Emerson or
Melville, Prometheus, but Emerson's own Uriel:

> And when he made so perilously bold
> As to be scattered forth in black and white,
> Good fathers looked askance at him and rolled
> Their inward eyes in anguish and affright;

> There were some of them did shake at what was told,
> And they shook best who knew that he was right.

Emerson, we recall, had ended "Uriel" by having all "truth-speaking things" in Nature confirm Uriel's radically humanistic, anti-authoritarian, and antinomian words, so that

> a blush tinged the upper sky,
> And the gods shook, they knew not why.

In Robinson's poem the "Good fathers" of the church are granted more insight than Emerson was willing to credit the old gods with; they *know* why, and shake all the more because they know: "And they shook best who knew that he was right."

"Erasmus" makes a typically Robinsonian comment on the sage who wrote "Uriel." Emersonian in sympathy though he was, the younger poet could not accept Emerson's wholly antinomian conclusions, just because he lacked faith in the religious basis of antinomianism. Unless the rebellious soul is really in contact with God, his denial of society's norms *ought* to be called seditious and subversive, as it always is. But suppose there *is* no God, or suppose there is no way of knowing anything about Him, as Herbert Spencer had said? Then antinomianism would seem to be only irresponsible idiosyncrasy.

Furthermore, though Robinson could go along with Emerson in describing himself as an "endless seeker," he could not at all agree with the way Emerson ended his description of himself, "with no past at my back." Despite his intellectual skepticism—"wavering commitment" might be a better description of it—Robinson now and all through his life was very much tied to the past. As he saw it, it was not that the past lacked insight into reality, but that such insights were denied to *us,* and there was no use our pretending to have them. "Erasmus" comments on the Reformation from a *Protestant* point of view, but there is nothing in it of the radical antinomianism of Emerson's poem. Robinson's affinity with Emerson was tempered both by his almost equally strong affinity with Hawthorne, and by his sense that transcendentalism was no longer really possible as a philosophy or as a way of life.

In the title poem of the volume, "Captain Craig," Robinson creates an aged Emerson whom he puts to tests more severe, as he supposes, than any that Emerson had faced, in order to watch the results. The Captain is dying and dependent on the charity of "five or six" young people who come to his room to hear him talk. One of the five or six, the speaker in the poem,

is the most sympathetic, indeed even a kind of "secret disciple" like the
Nicodemus of John's Gospel that Robinson would write about later; but
even he cannot fail to recognize, sadly, that for all his immense courtesy,
serenity, and benevolence, the Captain is something of a crank. Certainly
his unqualified claim to be speaking with the voice of God would seem
monstrous egotism in anyone less completely benevolent or less truly mod-
est, in his person if not his philosophy.

But perhaps more important than his courtesy and his benevolence in
keeping him from seeming a mere madman is his sense of humor. To ease
the embarrassment caused by his being at once the host and instructor of
his young friends, and the grateful recipient of their charity, the Captain
"makes game" of them, humorously overstating on one occasion the fundamental conviction by which he has lived:

> "You are the resurrection and the life,"
> He said, "and I the hymn the Brahmin sings,"

thus claiming for them identity with Christ and for himself identity with
Brahma, as pictured in Emerson's poem of that title.

Thus the Captain passes every test but one to which he and his philosophy are put. His actions—whatever "actions" a bedridden, dying mendi-
cant is capable of—are the proof of his words—for *him,* but perhaps for
him only. For all his magnificent talk, he never reveals the secret of his
confidence. That it is not simply the result of well-being and success is clear
to all his listeners, but what *is* its source? There is a curious cloudiness
about all the Captain's attempts to explain. He states at one time or another
almost every major Emersonian doctrine—except the one on which they all
ultimately rested, the mystical doctrine of "the way up," the soul's ascension
to God through Nature as the intuition and the imagination read Nature as
a symbolic language. Clearly, the Captain's firm belief that the ultimate pat-
tern of the universe is love has allowed him to preserve his serenity, but how
are the five or six to know that his belief is true? The one test he does *not*
pass, because he never even recognizes its existence, is the purely abstract
and intellectual one, the "evidential" one: How do we *know?*

The "I" of the poem, the "secret disciple," seems to have a glimmering
of how the Captain knows, but he never attempts to reduce his understanding to words. Is it his sense that the Captain's words are *true* that makes
him listen so intently and sympathetically while the others cough and doze?
Or could it be that the tie between them was not their sharing a knowledge
hidden from the others but simple gratitude? Explaining the Captain's superiority to a sense of sin and the need for repentance—the soul's mumps,

as Emerson had said—the speaker defines the Captain's self-chosen role this
way:

> No penitential shame for what had come,
> No virtuous regret for what had been,—
> But rather a joy to find it in his life
> To be an outcast usher of the soul
> For such as had good courage of the Sun
> To pattern Love.

This would remind us of the way Matthew Arnold had just characterized Emerson in his American lecture on him—as "the friend and aider of
those who would live in the spirit"—except for the "outcast" before "usher
of the soul." An "outcast" is one without status. Captain Craig himself can
hardly be called an outcast, unless every prophet and sage who rejects the
norms of his society, including its idea of what constitutes success, should
be so called. "Things are in the saddle and ride mankind," Emerson had
said, thus rejecting his society's practical materialism; but Emerson was no
outcast.

I suspect the word is used by the "I" of the poem to describe the Captain because the sage who had meant so much to Robinson several years
before had been, as a *philosopher,* cast out by the naturalism of the time,
deprived of philosophical status. If this is true, then the unexplained sympathy of the speaker with the Captain rests not on secret knowledge but on
secret gratitude. The basis of the gratitude could not be explained without
the speaker himself suffering loss of status. Robinson's decision to remove
Emerson's name from the sonnet praising him shows that he was becoming
sensitive to the charge of being an Emersonian. The charge would be, in
1902, in the eyes of his friend Henderson and many others, almost equivalent to being called a frustrated romantic, or a wishfully-thinking Idealist,
or even a mystagogue. Surely Robinson is speaking partly for himself, or at
least about what he feared *might* have happened to him had he not covered
his tracks so well, when he has the "I" of "Captain Craig" say that as a
result of his championship of the Captain,

> They loaded me with titles of odd form
> And unexemplified significance,
> Like "Bellows-mender to Prince Aeolus,"
> "Pipe-filler to the Hoboscholiast,"
> "Bread-fruit for the Non-Doing," with one more
> That I remember, and a dozen more
> That I forget.

I can't help wondering whether the "one more" remembered but not divulged may not have included the name of Emerson. At any rate, after *Captain Craig,* which could never have been written without Emerson, Robinson stopped writing his friends about Emerson's philosophy as a resource—until that last letter written from his deathbed. The reason, I suspect, was not any nervous compulsion to hide a "source" but a growing recognition that Emerson was no longer really useful to him as a resource. The darkness had seemed to be lifting, but now it closed in again. There *must* be a Purpose and a Law, as he was soon to write, but he now realized that Emerson, inspiring example though he remained, could not tell him *why* there "must." What I have called the covering of tracks certainly occurred, but the motive for it was partly Robinson's lack of confidence in his own thinking and partly a disillusion with the "master" considered as Sage. Hereafter the debt would be paid by tributes to Emerson the *poet.*

With relatively few exceptions, Robinson's best later poems contain no suggestion of his debt to Emerson. Even when they include muted suggestions of ideas that might be Emersonian, or at least vaguely transcendental, the *tone* is as completely un-Emersonian as it is possible to imagine any tone being. As Robert Frost said in his introduction to *King Jasper,* Robinson, in his best work at least, is the poet of "immedicable grief," whose theme—his real theme, whatever his intention—is "unhappiness itself." Though Robinson would not have thought this a fair or perceptive description of his work—and it does omit a number of fine poems—there is a sense in which Frost's characterization of the work ought to be thought of as a primary insight, needing to be qualified in a number of ways but not reversed.

The tone and atmosphere of Robinson's work as a whole are epitomized in the concluding lines of one of the poems first published in *The Children of the Night,* "The Clerks":

> What comes of all your visions and your fears?
> Poets and kings are but the clerks of Time,
> Tiering the same dull webs of discontent,
> Clipping the same sad alnage of the years.

A comparison of Emerson's "Monadnoc" with Robinson's much briefer and simpler "Monadnock through the Trees" would be a better way—because fairer to Robinson—of getting at the same point, his prevailing tone. Emerson's poem does not simply acknowledge, it strongly emphasizes, the mountain's *enduring* quality compared with man's brief span of life, and its indifference to the little men who live in its shadow; yet Emerson's tone is confident and positive, and the concluding lines affirm, as

we have seen, the centrality and permanence not only of life but of the
individual. When Robinson looked at the same mountain from Peterbor-
ough, he saw its pyramid as the shape of death and its "calm" endurance—
the quality that Emerson had stressed—dwarfing and diminishing life. The
resulting poem amounts to an elegy for all mankind:

> Before there was in Egypt any sound
> Of those who reared a more prodigious means
> For the self-heavy sleep of kings and queens
> Than hitherto had mocked the most renowned,—
> Unvisioned here and waiting to be found,
> Alone, amid remote and older scenes,
> You loomed above ancestral evergreens
> Before there were the first of us around.
>
> And when the last of us, if we know how,
> See farther from ourselves than we do now,
> Assured with other sight than heretofore
> That we have done our mortal best and worst,—
> Your calm will be the same as when the first
> Assyrians went howling south to war.

The elegiac effect of "Monadnock through the Trees" is conveyed more
briefly and more poignantly in one of Robinson's most memorable short
poems, "The Dark Hills":

> Dark hills at evening in the west,
> Where sunset hovers like a sound
> Of golden horns that sang to rest
> Old bones of warriors under ground,
> Far now from all the bannered ways
> Where flash the legions of the sun,
> You fade—as if the last of days
> Were fading, and all wars were done.

Robinson was quite right, of course, in his feeling that the First World
War, in the background of the poem, the "war to end war," would not be
the last of wars, that days would go on fading and the wars never be done,
but it is not as sad prognostication that the poem is chiefly impressive. The
lines express a grief too pure to be lightened by any merely historical
change, an "immedicable" grief, as Frost said. Life itself, the poem implies,

is like a war in which defeat is inevitable; with or without the wars of nations, we are all of us Rolands fighting a doomed rearguard action in a narrow pass, only for us there are no "golden horns" to sing us under ground.

That Robinson himself would have denied—*did* deny, repeatedly— that any such statement as this was a fair summary of his *belief*, is not to the point. This is the way he tended to *feel* about life. Against the feeling, he could oppose only a set of beliefs for which he could find almost no support. The result was that a good many of his poems are weakened by the incompatibility of their emotional tone and their explicit statements of belief. It is not at all surprising that Robinson's first reviewer found the atmosphere of *The Torrent and the Night Before* to be like that of a "prison-house." He was anticipating Frost's reaction to all the later work—and not only Frost's, but that of what seems to be the majority of Robinson's critics. He was responding to a palpable atmosphere, to the work as *poetry*, in short, rather than to the many direct expressions of Emersonian idealism sprinkled through it.

This disparity between sensibility and belief that runs through so much of his work, particularly that part of it which attempts in any degree to be philosophical, probably has more to do with the preference of most readers for the early Tilbury Town portraits than any other factor. In the best of these studies of failure and alienation, the art is marvelously controlled. In the very best, there is a strong identification between the character in the poem and Robinson himself, or someone closely identified with him, leading to a balance Robinson could not always maintain between pity and humor. "Mr. Flood's Party" clearly reflects Robinson's own experience with liquor consumed in vast quantities as an anodyne, and "Eros Turannos," which may well be Robinson's greatest short poem, clearly reflects his hopeless and tragic love for the incredibly beautiful Emma, brother Herman's wife. But "Miniver Cheevy" is probably the most instructive example of a subject that permitted Robinson to write at his best level in the Tilbury Town poems.

Miniver is the archetypal frustrated romantic idealist, born in the wrong time for idealism. He is close enough to being Robinson himself so that Robinson can smile at him and let the pathos remain unspoken.

> Miniver Cheevy, child of scorn,
>   Grew lean while he assailed the seasons.
> He wept that he was ever born,
>   And he had reasons.

Here and throughout the poem the relation between what Miniver knows and what the speaker knows is subtle and effective. Miniver wept and the poet does not weep, but not because he thinks there are no *reasons* to weep. Robinson knew too much about the reasons for an idealist to weep to permit him to make Miniver a mere butt of humor. Apart from his intellectual reasons, which I have already said enough about, there were more personal and emotional ones that are relevant to any discussion of Robinson's identification with Miniver Cheevy. Robinson was born the third son of a family whose hearts were so set on having a daughter this time that they had made no provisions for the name of an unwanted son. For more than six months the boy remained unnamed, until strangers at a summer resort, feeling that he ought to be granted an identity beyond that of simply "the baby," put slips of paper with male first names written on them into a hat and chose someone to draw one out. The man who drew out the slip with "Edwin" written on it happened to live in Arlington, Massachusetts, which seemed to provide the easiest choice for a second name; and so by an "accident of fate," we have a poet named Edwin Arlington Robinson. Robinson hated the name and thought of himself as a child of scorn—and he had reasons.

> Miniver sighed for what was not,
>   And dreamed, and rested from his labors;
> He dreamed of Thebes and Camelot,
>   And Priam's neighbors.
>
> Miniver mourned the ripe renown
>   That made so many a name so fragrant;
> He mourned Romance, now on the town,
>   And Art, a vagrant.

Like Miniver too, Robinson "dreamed of Camelot"—and wrote three very long, and very tedious, Arthurian poems in which the "dreaming" is compulsive and unrecognized. But in "Miniver Cheevy" the dreaming is compulsive only for Miniver, not for the poet. Who would *not* turn to the past for his values if he lived in an age when the "facts" of coldly objective knowledge seemed to leave no room for any "ideal" values and when a "mere poet" who made no money was considered a failure by Tilbury Town's standards? For Romance to be "on the town" meant for it to be the object of the township's charity, in the poor farm or on home relief; in either case the object not only of "charity" but of the scorn that would accompany it. "Vagrants"—tramps—would sometimes spend a few days or weeks "on the town" before wandering on. The connection between Miniver and Emerson comes through Captain Craig, who was also described as a "vagrant" and was also the object of charity; for the penniless philosopher of the earlier poem was not, as critics have so often said, Robinson himself but Emerson *in extremis*.

> Miniver scorned the gold he sought,
>   But sore annoyed was he without it;
> Miniver thought, and thought, and thought,
>   And thought about it.
>
> Miniver Cheevy, born too late,
>   Scratched his head and kept on thinking;
> Miniver coughed, and called it fate,
>   And kept on drinking.

But unlike the Captain, Miniver *is* Robinson, or at least that part of Robinson that Robinson recognized as being romantic and idealistic. He too had "thought, and thought, and thought, / And thought about it," without arriving at any conclusions definite enough to be stated very clearly, even to himself. He too had resented his poverty while condemning practical materialism and popular notions of success. He too had "called it fate" and for many years "kept on drinking." A good deal of the time he was almost as convinced as Miniver that he had been "born too late."

It should be unnecessary to say that such a lining-up of the parallels between Robinson and his character is no substitute for a close critical analysis of the ways in which the poem works. My purpose in calling attention to the analogy is twofold: first, to illustrate the earlier generalization that Robinson wrote at his best level in the Tilbury Town poems when he wrote about a projection of an aspect of himself; and second, to prepare the way for a further conclusion, namely, that the side of himself that Robinson could stand off from and smile at was the *believing* side, never the deeper self that felt only the grief. So that the lack of any *direct* expression of his transcendentalism in most of his best poems—"Captain Craig" excepted—does not mean that his debt to Emerson is confined to a few early minor works. Emerson remained indirectly useful to his art even while he failed the man. When Robinson finally got to the point where he could be amused at beliefs that had once seemed capable of saving him from despair, he transformed frustrations into some of our finest poems.

The tragedy of Robinson's career was his failure to develop beyond the

level of achievement he reached very early—in *Captain Craig* in 1902, and
for short poems, in *The Man against the Sky* in 1916. It is doubtful that he
ever again wrote so fine a long poem as "Isaac and Archibald," in the *Captain Craig* volume, which strikes me as much greater than the long character
studies of back-country New Englanders that Robert Frost would shortly
do. And the title poem of the volume seems to me very much better than the
infrequent and generally slighting comment on it would lead one to expect.
As for the short poems, surely he never excelled "Miniver Cheevy" in *The
Town down the River* in 1910, unless it was in "Hillcrest" or "Eros Turannos" in *The Man against the Sky*. The general opinion that the very long
poems on which he spent most of his time after 1916 are for the most part
quite unreadable needs a little qualifying but is not basically mistaken. Why
did Robinson fail to develop?

The worst of the long poems are undoubtedly the Arthurian legends
and the earlier long narratives of modern life. Most of them have patches
of good writing, to be sure. Robinson himself thought he had never written
better than in the concluding lines of *Tristram*, and it is true that in them he
does bring grief and despair to quintessential expression. But in general the
combined prolixity and obscurity of these poems make them not worth
reading or rereading. Words at this point in his career seem to have become
a way of blotting out time with Robinson, as though he were not writing
poems but playing solitaire and hoping the game might last as long as possible. He is using words in these poems not to reveal but to delay or obscure
meaning.

The only conspicuous exceptions to this statement in the period between *The Man against the Sky* and *Cavender's House* in 1929 are the Biblical poems, "The Three Taverns" and "Lazarus," both included in *The
Three Taverns* in 1920. Just why these are so very much better than the
other long poems of the period is still anybody's guess. Of course, they are
not so long as the others, for one thing. But their superiority is not simply
negative. My own guess is that Robinson's sympathies were more fully engaged here and his imagination stirred, but it is also true that the Biblical
stories he expanded seemed to him to contain their own meanings, so that
he was not under the necessity of philosophizing, an activity that he was
now incapable of, as almost every new long poem made clearer. The *narrative* structure had been supplied in the Arthurian tales, to be sure, but not
the *meaning*. When he returned to Biblical narrative in *Nicodemus* in 1932,
he produced another of his best long poems.

Now he had something like the special advantage he had had in "Miniver Cheevy," the advantage of combined sympathetic identification and distance that had enabled him in that poem to understand Miniver as Miniver understood himself, yet also smile as one who knew more than Miniver. For increasingly in these last years Robinson himself was a sort of "secret disciple" like Nicodemus, who visited Jesus at night to ask how a man might be born again. But his discipleship was not to an orthodox Christ so much as to a blend of Emerson, Christ, and Buddha. So that in this poem not only the narrative (as in the Arthurian poems) but the meaning and the point of view were *supplied* him.

The partial recovery of control that occurred in the last half dozen years of Robinson's life amounted to a kind of return to what he had tried to do in prose drama in *Van Zorn* and *The Porcupine* in 1914 and 1915. So far as it is possible to tell from reading Robinson's critics and the literary historians, no one appears to have read these plays for the past fifty years, but they are very much more worth reading than most of the long poems that pad the *Collected Poems* to its forbidding length of 1488 pages of small print. Whether they are "good theater" or not I will not even try to guess, but certainly they are good reading.

Van Zorn: A Comedy in Three Acts seems to me the less credible of the two, but even it has its points. Adapting itself to the conventions of drawing-room comedy of the time, it strongly anticipates Eliot's *The Cocktail Party* in its reliance on a wise and mysterious benefactor who brings about a cure of souls partly by helping the lost children to discover what they are and want and partly by events he arranges to have happen. The only important difference between Eliot's psychiatrist and Robinson's "Flying Dutchman" Van Zorn is that the psychiatrist is part of a group of the enlightened who work with him closely, a church in short, while Van Zorn works entirely alone. This is what should be expected from the differing theological backgrounds of the two plays. Eliot's play is explicitly Christian, Robinson's vaguely oriental, or at least a sort of amalgam of Christianity and Buddhism.

The hero who is turned to the light and given a second birth by the influence of the redemptive Van Zorn is sometimes jokingly called Phoebus Apollo, or light and wisdom, and sometimes "Old Hundred,"—"Praise God from whom all blessings flow . . . Praise Father, Son, and Holy Ghost," the hymn adapted from the one hundredth Psalm. In either case, he has some sort of special relation to God—or *is* God. As wisdom and light, he is the God within, frustrated, suffering, "drinking too much"; as "Old Hundred" he is a sort of Christ-figure. When he gives up drinking, he says he has been "born again" and is said by others to be "illuminated"; and after this there is a good deal of play on *light*, once again anticipating *The Cocktail Party*.

Van Zorn himself is called a "fatalist" and said to have an "Oriental" way with him—unusual, surely, in a Dutch millionaire. He is also said to have "mirrors" into which he can look, so that perhaps the wisdom he helps the others to attain is really self-knowledge, which would be a way to salvation close enough to Buddhism to justify the "Oriental" epithet. The universal compassion and feeling for destiny that emerge from the play as felt rather than from stated themes are also of course oriental—which fact does not prevent them from being at the same time gifts to Robinson from Emerson, who himself in middle and later years was much attracted to the Orient.

The Porcupine even more clearly looks back to Emerson and the "oriental reading" Robinson did in the 1890s, and just as clearly points forward to Eliot's later plays. In its use of a redemptive character with the power to change people's lives, it suggests *The Cocktail Party,* as *Van Zorn* does, but in its concern with the relation of self-knowledge to vocation, it looks toward Eliot's *The Confidential Clerk.* In its emphasis on growth beyond one's earlier "self," it suggests Eliot's "Fare forward, voyager," of *The Four Quartets.* Larry, the redemptive character, says at one point,

> Yes, Rachel, that's just about what we are—children. The best and the worst, the wisest and the silliest of us—children. Tumbling, blundering, groping children,—getting our heads bumped and our fingers burned, and making ourselves generally uncomfortable. But all this needn't keep us from growing, or from looking now and then as if we had not committed the unpardonable sin in being born.

I think we may see in *The Porcupine*'s theme of growth or death—the one who is called "the porcupine" develops protective quills, refuses to grow, and ends by suicide—some remnant of Robinson's legacy from Emerson, though there is nothing specifically Emersonian in the language of the play. But whether there is any actual influence of Emerson on the play or not, is not really the point. Like *Van Zorn* it gives us a Robinson writing clearly and coherently, interestingly and pointedly, of the elements of his faith that, woven together, gave him whatever hope he had. With no attempt to reason systematically, as he would soon try to do in "The Man against the Sky," these two plays taken together give us a much better idea of what his "philosophy" came to be than the poem does. Of the poem, he once wrote an inquirer that he considered it his best statement of his "philosophy—as you choose to call it." Both the aesthetic failure of the poem itself and the qualification attached to this statement about it suggest the failure of the long semiphilosophical narratives that were soon to follow.

In *Amaranth* and *King Jasper,* his last two poems, the writing becomes clearer than it had been for years, the prolixity diminishes, and the stories *move.* The themes are the by now familiar ones of finding the true self and the true vocation, the danger and the promise of growth, and the search for the light. In both we meet again the wise guide, the disseminator of true knowledge, who makes one know oneself, the semisupernatural teacher. In both, the end sought is the wisdom that makes it possible for us to accept change and to grow. It is hard to say whether the two poems should be called more Buddhist or more Emersonian.

Amaranth is completely Hawthornesque in its form, and chiefly Emersonian I should say, though also oriental, in its meaning. A dream-allegory of life in a hell of illusion where there is no knowledge of the true self, it ends for Fargo—who will, we guess, go far—in an awakening that brings new hope and a burst of light—

> While he spoke,
> The world around him flamed amazingly
> With light that comforted and startled him
> With joy, and with ineffable release.
> There was a picture of unrolling moments
> In a full morning light.

King Jasper glances at the social problems of revolution in the 1930s, with unyielding Capitalism and destructive Communism apparently equally to be deplored; but its real center is the problem of change and growth once again. Zoë, whom Robinson defined for an inquirer as not life but knowledge, is the life-giving wisdom that comes to those who maintain their contact with the eternities. Robinson hints allegorically, but with sufficient clarity so that one would have thought that the inquirer would not have needed to inquire, she is to be thought of as one of the daughters of Proteus, the Old Man of the Sea. She comes into the castle of the industrial magnate, the "King" of the present world, offering freedom and new life, but neither the King nor his Queen is able to face newness, and in the end, after they have committed suicide and their son, who has understood and loved her, has been destroyed by the materialist revolutionary, Zoë is alone with her secret and saving knowledge. Despite the suicide and slaughter of all the ordinary human characters in the poem, the ending is intended, I think, to express a hope that others may find and love Zoë.

One difference between these two long poems and the earlier ones is their frank use of allegory. Most of the earlier ones, even in the Arthurian cycle, were "realistic" without seeming "real." Another difference is the greater hopefulness of them, especially of *Amaranth*. But what strikes me as the really significant difference is that in them Robinson is no longer just maundering, piling up distinctions without a difference or making affirmations that affirm nothing more solid than that affirmations are much to be desired. The poems have their defects, to be sure, some of which are implied in the preceding summaries, but the defects are not crippling. The poems deserve a better fate than to go unread, as they have for so many years. Like the plays, that have gone unread even longer, they give us a Robinson who has something worth saying, who knows what it is, and who goes about saying it with sufficient power and relevance to our interests to make it well worth our time to read them.

There are many ways to tell the story of Robinson's career. To approach him chiefly through a study of his relations with Emerson, as I have just done, is of course simply one of them. Some years ago I told the same story more briefly from the vantage point of Robinson's knowledge of science and scientific philosophy, its effect on him, and his attempts to refute some of its implications. The conclusions I arrived at then were not strikingly different from those that have emerged in my writing this time. It seemed from that earlier vantage point that Robinson was damaged as a poet, kept from developing his special gifts as he might have, by his excessive preoccupation with the "materialism" of science, which forced a man with no gifts for abstract thought to try to be a poetic philosopher.

The story should be told some time from the standpoint of Robinson's relations with *both* of his favorite American writers, who were also Dickinson's—Hawthorne and Emerson. His responses to the two were very different, especially in the formative years of his career. His first response to Emerson, as we have seen, was to a sage who might provide comfort in time of trouble, and at no time does his early interpretation of the sage seem particularly acute. He seems at first not really to have confronted the problem of epistemology, the problem created by the fact that the metaphysic of Idealism rested upon a theory of how and what we *know*. He at first appears to have tried to accept Idealism without accepting the theory of knowledge that supported it.

Some degree of awareness of the difficulty of this maneuver must have been present to Robinson even from the beginning, though, for his attempt to find support for Emersonian Idealism in Eastern religion was essentially an attempt to fill in what seemed to him a gap in Emerson, to give Emerson's thought the foundation it seemed to him to lack. Thus when in "The Sage" he describes Emerson as having developed his philosophy by going back to ancient oriental truth for his wisdom, he is being inaccurate about Emerson historically, and certainly misinterpreting the early transcendental Emerson; but he is also instinctively repeating Emerson's own development, for Emerson himself, as the ecstatic moments of awareness came less and less frequently, leaned increasingly on the support he found in oriental religion. What both the late Emerson and Robinson tended to omit in their response to oriental teaching was the element best represented in Zen Buddhism, the concentration on full awareness of the concrete actual event or object—the *actual* perceived in such depth as to reveal the indwelling eternal spirit. Thus once again Robinson tended to miss the way of *knowing* on which the conclusions rested, as he had when he drew on Emerson.

The Emerson of Robinson's plays and late poems is an evolutionary theist who makes no mystical claims, who only calls for continued growth or self-transcendence, for the superiority of individual over societal claims, and for acceptance of one's destiny. Here it seems to me Robinson's understanding of the later Emerson who had appealed to him *was* acute. Emerson so interpreted is a very substantial figure, however far he may be from the more exciting Emerson of the early poems and lectures. The substantial quality of his thought accounts for a considerable part of the value of Robinson's plays and latest long poems.

Robinson responded to Hawthorne surely and acutely from the very beginning, not as a sage but as an artist. His kinship with the older writer was temperamental, not philosophic, a shared response of the whole sensibility to experience, not the satisfaction of a need for belief. The only thing he missed in his aesthetic response to Hawthorne was the "light" that Hawthorne wanted to affirm, and sometimes did affirm, more or less successfully. But if, as it seems to me, Hawthorne himself felt the darkness of experience more strongly and instinctively than he felt the light, then it is not surprising that Robinson, responding as an artist to an artist, should have sensed primarily the "blackness" there that Melville had noted long before. Robinson found in Hawthorne a great writer who was a kindred spirit.

Unfortunately, in *Amaranth,* where Hawthorne's presence is most apparent, it is the Hawthorne of the allegorical sketches like "The Great Carbuncle" and "The Christmas Banquet," not the Hawthorne of the less abstract tales, who is primarily evident. *Cavender's House* is less obviously Hawthornesque but the Hawthorne we find in it is better Hawthorne. The house is an image of the mind, and as Cavender explores its dark rooms, searching for he knows not what, he confronts his own deeper self, its guilt primarily, but its innocence too. The two themes of the poem, that the answers to our most urgent questions cannot be given us from outside ourselves but must be found within, and that when we stand in the darkness we are better able to see the light, are good Hawthorne as well as good Robinson. *Cavender's House* is one of the more rewarding of the long poems.

Robinson was much closer in his style, everywhere in his work, to Hawthorne than to Emerson. He seldom *sounds* like Emerson, but very often like Hawthorne. His preference for traditional meters and stanzaic forms, his diction, and especially his hesitant, tentative rhythms, draw him as close, perhaps, to Hawthorne as verse can ever come to prose. Both artists were men with the strongest feeling for ancient pieties and traditional verities; both had an instinctive sense that the more everything changed, the more it was the same; both felt shut out from the warmth of life by conditions within them, for which they blamed sometimes fate and sometimes themselves.

All this and more that is so important in Robinson's work has necessarily received scant recognition in a treatment in which Emerson has provided the focus. But not everything can be said at once. The focus provided by Emerson has had the advantage, as I hope, of throwing more light on two matters that seem to me greatly in need of being lighted up than an approach to Robinson through Hawthorne would have. The first of these is Robinson's place in the *tradition* of American poetry, the question, for instance, of where he stands in relation to Dickinson and Frost. The second is the problem created by his failure to develop, as Dickinson did and Frost would, when his literary resources were so much like hers and when he shared with Frost a major debt to Emerson. From this point of view the primary question is not how he succeeded—on *this,* Hawthorne could throw much light—but why he failed as much as he did.

Perhaps he himself pointed toward the answer when he thought of himself as born in the wrong time—the wrong time at any rate for a man of sensibility who was inclined to be an Emersonian Idealist.

NATHAN COMFORT STARR

The Transformation of Merlin

The sage and enchanter Merlin, especially as we find him in Edwin Arlington Robinson's poem *Merlin,* is a striking example of the change and
development in the Arthurian legend from the very beginning. During the
twentieth century he has been more originally portrayed than ever before.
First, however, let us briefly survey his past history.

He first appears in Nennius's *Historia Brittonum* (ca. 800) as Ambrosius, a boy born without a father, who reveals miraculous powers of divination to King Vortigern. Geoffrey of Monmouth's *Historia Regum Britanniae* (1136) expanded Nennius's account, renaming the boy Ambrosius
Merlinus, and telling of Arthur's birth, who was conceived through Merlin's
enchantment. The seventh chapter of Geoffrey's *Historia* consists of the
prophecies of Merlin, a confusing series of predictions, many of dire disasters. Geoffrey also wrote the *Vita Merlini,* which describes the strange career of a Merlin not associated with Arthur, the so-called Caledonian Merlin, Merlinus Silvestris. Both of these works by Geoffrey foreshadow the
dimension later found in the twentieth-century seer. Successive reworkings
of the *Historia Regum Britanniae* by Wace and Layamon add greatly to
Merlin's importance as Arthur's adviser.

In the thirteenth-century Vulgate romance, *L'Estoire de Merlin,* the
seer is even more important. As a two-year-old child he had dictated to the
clerk Blaise an account of Joseph of Arimathea and the Holy Grail. He is
responsible for the early nurture of Arthur, and had proposed to Arthur's
father, Uther Pendragon, the establishment of the Round Table. After Ar-

From *Edwin Arlington Robinson: Centenary Essays,* edited by Ellsworth Barnard.
© 1969 by the University of Georgia Press.

thur is chosen king by the test of the sword in the anvil Merlin advises him to marry Guinevere, and plays a important role in wars against the rebellious kings and the Saxons. Eventually he meets Viviane, who induces him to reveal his secrets of magic and imprisons him in the forest of Broceliande.

Malory, who based the *Morte D'Arthur* in large part on the Vulgate romances, enhanced Merlin's function as a seer and magician by a number of important prophecies, including a prediction of his own end. He gives valuable advice to Arthur, takes him to a lake where he receives the sword Excalibur, and shows great skill as a shape-shifter. Malory's account of Merlin's imprisonment by Nyneve is lively and circumstantial.

> Then the lady and Merlyon departed. And by weyes he shewed hir many wondyrs, and so come into Cornuayle. And all wayes he lay aboute to have hir maydenhode, and she was ever passynge wery of hym and wolde have bene delyverde of hym, for she was aferde of hym for cause he was a devyls son, and she cowde not be skyfte of hym by no meane. And so one a tyme Merlyon ded shew hir in a roche whereas was a grete wondir and wrought by enchauntement that went undir a grete stone. So by hir subtyle worching she made Merlyon to go undir that stone to latte hir wete of the mervayles there, but she wrought so there for hym that he come never oute for all the craufte he coude do, and so she departed and leffte Merlyon.

The contrast between this imprisonment and that of Robinson's Merlin could scarcely be more striking. The later seer is "imprisoned" by the fascination of an unusually gifted woman, not by enchantment.

After the publication of the *Morte D'Arthur* the fortunes of Merlin suffered in the general decline of the Arthurian legend until the return of Malory to favor in the nineteenth century. Even so, Merlin was not distinguished. The ill-tempered old humbug of Mark Twain's *Connecticut Yankee* was a grotesque figure, and even Tennyson's Merlin, in the *Idyll* "Vivien," was a learned old fool, at the mercy of a predatory, shallow wanton. He seemed to have been imprisoned more by Tennyson than Vivien. In a welcome revision of the traditional story, however, he was released from bondage by the publication of Robinson's *Merlin* in 1917.

Before we go further it is well worth noting that at least three writers after Robinson's time also greatly increased Merlin's importance. Robinson seems not to have influenced any of them; in all likelihood they were the inheritors of the exploratory, expansive temper of the time, especially of inquiries into the mysterious capacities of the human mind. At any rate a new Merlin has come into the legend.

Charles Williams, in his distinguished cycle of Arthurian poems, *Taliessin through Logres* (1938) and *The Region of the Summer Stars* (1944), describes Merlin as a supernatural force acting for Christian ends. He and his sister Brisen, the son and daughter of Nimue (a striking change from the old relationship), live in the wood of Broceliande, where inchoate forces are working for the creation of forms. Merlin is called Time (compare Robinson's Merlin, and Time) and Brisen is Space. Merlin helps Arthur come to the throne and is the means by which Galahad is conceived. Most important of all, it is his mission to assist Arthur in establishing the holy kingdom of Logres. In Williams's poems we are conscious of a vastly enlarged world, not only of sense, but of the region of the summer stars, of the "Third Heaven," the abode of "the feeling intellect," as the author says in a borrowing from Wordsworth.

Laurence Binyon's *The Madness of Merlin,* published posthumously in 1947 and never completed, was based mainly on Geoffrey of Monmouth's *Vita Merlini.* That being the case, Binyon's Merlin, Merlinus Sylvestris, is not the usual enchanter. His world is vast and terrible. Even as a boy he was set apart. His sister Gwyndeth says of him:

> I remember how, but a boy,
> Suddenly he would seem a stranger among us.
> As if he had wandered out in a strange land
> Seeing us no more; and then as suddenly
> His spirit would return to the use of the body;
> But to none told he ever in what land he had been.
> Now, as I guess,
> It was some blinding vision from above
> Estranged the world to him.

Like Geoffrey's, Binyon's Merlin is ridden by terror. He does not have the solace of Christianity as in Williams, or the "Light" which shines, even though faintly, in Robinson's Camelot. Yet again these Merlins are kin, members of the doomed band of men who see too much.

Finally there is C. S. Lewis's Merlinus Ambrosius, in his novel *That Hideous Strength* (1947), a tale of England after the Second World War, in which malign spirits from outer space try to degrade and destroy mankind. Merlinus has lain buried for many centuries in a state of suspended animation, but finally rises and joins in the destruction of the evil force. Lewis explains that he is able to give his aid to a small group of dedicated Christians because he represents immemorially old supernatural power, "Atlantean" magic. Again this Merlin is far removed from the conventional magician and seer. Like Williams's Merlin his ancient home might well have been the region of the summer stars.

Let us return, however, to Robinson. His concept of the poem *Merlin* and the world view which it embodied ensured great breadth for the story. It was written during the First World War, a disaster which caused Robinson again and again to express apocalyptic premonitions of doom facing the world. The tale of Arthur and the tragic fall of his kingdom had gripped his imagination since boyhood; now the destruction of Camelot seemed to him all too like the decay of twentieth-century civilization.

Arthur's realm was tottering to its ruin, rent asunder by the selfishness and violence of the knights of the Round Table and by the cancerous adultery of Lancelot and Guinevere. Merlin finds himself almost immobilized by divided loyalties to Arthur and Vivian. Lancelot and Guinevere cannot give up their love, and Arthur is powerless either to acknowledge or correct the situation. Robinson's description of Arthur's agony of mind is deeply moving.

> he saw giants rising in the dark,
> Born horribly of memories and new fears
> That in the gray-lit irony of dawn
> Were partly to fade out and be forgotten;
> And then there might be sleep, and for a time
> There might again be peace. His head was hot
> And throbbing; but the rest of him was cold,
> As he lay staring hard where nothing stood,
> And hearing what was not, even while he saw
> And heard, like dust and thunder far away,
> The coming confirmation of the words
> Of him who saw so much and feared so little
> Of all that was to be. No spoken doom
> That ever chilled the last night of a felon
> Prepared a dragging anguish more profound
> And absolute than Arthur, in these hours,
> Made out of darkness and of Merlin's words;
> No tide that ever crashed on Lyonesse
> Drove echoes inland that were lonelier
> For widowed ears among the fisher-folk,

> Than for the King were memories tonight
> Of old illusions that were dead forever.

Arthur's helplessness finds its counterpart in the entrapment of Merlin between two obligations: his newfound identification with youth and beauty in Vivian and his position as Arthur's adviser. Arthur sees clearly the disastrous conflict in Merlin.

> "Men change in Brittany, Merlin," said the King;
> And even his grief had strife to freeze again
> A dreary smile for the transmuted seer
> Now robed in heavy wealth of purple silk,
> With frogs and foreign tassles. On his face,
> Too smooth now for a wizard or a sage,
> Lay written, for the King's remembering eyes,
> A pathos of a lost authority
> Long faded, and unconscionably gone;
> And on the King's heart lay a sudden cold.

Merlin's authority, his occupation, like Othello's, is gone. He is like the person in Robinson's "The Man against the Sky," published the year before *Merlin:*

> mounting with infirm unsearching tread,
> His hopes to chaos led,
> He may have stumbled up there from the past,
> And with an aching strangeness viewed the last
> Abysmal conflagration of his dreams.

Robinson's preoccupation with men faced by agonizing difficulties, losses of direction, failures of will, and paralyzing disillusionments finds powerful expression in his treatment of Merlin, giving him a dimension he almost never had before. Like Annandale

> Astray
> Out of his life and in another life;
> And in the stillness of this other life
> He wondered and he drowsed.

Yet Merlin's problem is vaster than Annandale's and his vision is more searching. Like Clavering he saw "too far for guidance of today"; yet unlike him he never saw "too near for the eternities." Robinson stresses Merlin's prophetic vision. In speaking of the Grail to Arthur he says,

> "I saw
> Too much, and that was never good for man.
> The man who goes alone too far goes mad—
> In one way or another."

And after Vivian leaves him for a time he tells himself,

> "The man who sees
> May see too far, and he may see too late
> The path he takes unseen."

Of all the characters in *Merlin* Vivian is the most original. She is a believable and intelligently conceived woman, no vulgar wanton as in Tennyson, no ambitious amateur in magic as in Malory, but an unusually fascinating and capable person, entangled in a difficulty far more troublesome than a love affair between a young woman and an older man. Vivian is no longer simply a seductress, finally extracting the secrets of Merlin's magic and condemning him to a perpetual imprisonment. Like Dalila she is involved in a national emergency. While Merlin lingers with her Arthur has to meet terrible difficulties in his crumbling kingdom without the counsel of his trusted sage. Arthur has been fully warned of Merlin's fate.

> Ten years ago
> The King had heard, with unbelieving ears
> At first, what Merlin said would be the last
> Reiteration of his going down
> To find a living grave in Brittany:
> "Buried alive I told you I should be,
> By love made little and by woman shorn,
> Like Samson, of my glory; and the time
> Is now at hand."

The tragic dimension of the story and the dilemma of Merlin himself—another Samson—is revealed in the twin imperatives of Broceliande and Camelot. Contrary to the opinion of some critics the two strands unite to make a single story of the conflict of virtually irreconcilable forces.

Like her predecessors Vivian is determined, against all the pressures from Camelot, to get what she wants. Again like her sisters, this seems not to be sensual delight—though she is by no means insensitive to it and appreciates physical attractiveness enough to make Merlin shave his beard—rather it is Merlin's *wisdom* that she seeks. But in a departure from earlier versions it is not his incantations that she wishes; like her predecessors she

is a relentlessly ambitious woman, but unlike them she has a good mind
which she wants to improve. As she says to Merlin,

> "When this great Merlin comes to me,
> My task and avocation for some time
> Will be to make him willing, if I can,
> To teach and feed me with an ounce of wisdom."

Vivian's lively, original mind is evident throughout the poem. She has a
degree of self-knowledge which puts her far above her predecessors. As she
says, she is cruel and cold and likes snakes. Volatile as quicksilver, she has
no set, inflexible attitudes. Though the first visit of Merlin frightens her, she
receives him with frankness and informality. Expressing hatred easily—she
hates King Arthur and she poisons those she hates—she is also capable of
giving Merlin a kind of love he has never known, adoration for his greatness, and deep affection. To her Merlin is a means of self-realization in the
fullest sense. As she says,

> "In an age
> That has no plan for me that I can read
> Without him, shall he tell me what I am,
> And why I am, I wonder?"

Later in Merlin's first visit she gains a deeper perception.

> "You are the wisest man that ever was,
> And I've a prayer to make: May all you say
> To Vivian be a part of what you knew
> Before the curse of her unquiet head
> Was on your shoulder, as you have it now,
> To punish you for knowing beyond knowledge.
> You are the only one who sees enough
> To make me see how far away I am
> From all that I have seen and have not been;
> You are the only thing there is alive
> Between me as I am and as I was
> When Merlin was a dream. You are to listen
> When I say now to you that I'm alone.
> Like you, I saw too much; and unlike you
> I made no kingdoms out of what I saw—
> Or none save this one here that you must rule,
> Believing you are ruled. I see too far

> To rule myself. Time's way with you and me
> Is our way, in that we are out of Time
> And out of tune with Time."

Possibly Robinson's greatest achievement in creating the character of Vivian lies in providing Merlin, as never before, with a woman who can not only satisfy the craving of his lost youth for beauty but who can also stimulate him intellectually. This stimulation is shown in passages like the one just quoted and in Vivian's angry reproach when Merlin tells her he must return again to Camelot. It is apparent also in practically every exchange between the two, in the deference which Merlin pays to a creature of mind as well as body.

There is another aspect of Vivian that makes her very real, and likable: her common sense. Merlin's "imprisonment" is not an imprisonment at all; Vivian tells him quite clearly that he is not supposed to dance attendance upon her. He should roam by himself as he pleases in complete freedom. What better way to complete Merlin's infatuation?

For a man who never married and who apparently never had a fully-satisfying love affair Robinson knows a great deal about women. The ladies in his Arthurian poems, Vivian, Guinevere, and Isolt, usually outshine the men. It is not that Merlin is weak by comparison: he is simply less original, less various, less flexible than Vivian. She is a very real person. The sage's imprisonment through incantation is gone; his "jailer" is a woman of flesh and blood—and mind.

Now as to Merlin himself. The gate-keeper Blaise, when Merlin reproaches him for the "vicious" and noisy gate to Broceliande, replies,

> "There's a way out of every wilderness
> For those who dare or care enough to find it."

The irony of this remark is immediately apparent. Merlin was indeed free to leave Broceliande when he wished; what he could never escape from was the "wilderness" of his dual obligations. This conflict, unlike Vivian's single purpose, adds great intensity to Robinson's Merlin. Early in the poem Gawaine says of him, in Broceliande, that he "wears the valiance of an ageless youth / Crowned with a glory of eternal peace." Yet Gawaine was wrong on both counts; his judgments were too capricious to be trusted. Merlin's "ageless youth" was factitious; his "eternal peace" a mockery.

The poignance of Merlin's dilemma, combined with the vivid originality of Vivian, gives new breadth and depth to the legend. It might be easy to assume, from the theme of Nemesis in the poem (as Arthur said of Merlin, his "Nemesis had made of him a slave") that the sage does nothing but let events take their course. This is not the case. He acts vigorously a number of times. After his first visit to Broceliande, for example, he reproaches Arthur as "a slack, blasted, and sad-fronted man"; he also warns the King against Mordred, and bids him not to let his enemies take the Queen and kingdom. Moreover, he is a free agent; he leaves Broceliande when he wishes, and he returns to Camelot the last time in agony of mind to do what he can for Arthur's realm. When he tells Vivian of the dangerous state of affairs in Camelot she reproaches him bitterly in a powerful scene. Merlin is in despair. Yet his place is in Camelot.

> A melancholy wave of revelation
> Broke over Merlin like a rising sea,
> Long viewed unwillingly and long denied.
> He saw what he had seen, but would not feel,
> Till now the bitterness of what he felt
> Was in his throat, and all the coldness of it
> Was on him and around him like a flood
> Of lonelier memories than he had said
> Were memories, although he knew them now
> For what they were—for what his eyes had seen,
> For what his ears had heard and what his heart
> Had felt, with him not knowing what it felt.
> But now he knew that his cold angel's name
> Was Change, and that a mightier will than his
> Or Vivian's had ordained that he be there.
> To Vivian he could not say anything
> But words that had no more of hope in them
> Than anguish had of peace: "I meant the world . . .
> I meant the world," he groaned; "not you—not me."

Later Merlin comes to terms with his destiny, in what is perhaps the most moving passage in the poem, a soliloquy charged with the imminence of death, indeed with the burial of his "poor blundering bones," and yet also illumined by courageous acceptance of what must be, and by the "light" which leads him:

> "let the man
> Who saw too much, and was to drive himself
> From paradise, play too lightly or too long
> Among the moths and flowers, he finds at last

There is a dim way out; and he shall grope
Where pleasant shadows lead him to the plain
That has no shadow save his own behind him.
And there, with no complaint, nor much regret,
Shall he plod on, with death between him now
And the far light that guides him, till he falls
And has an empty thought of empty rest;
Then Fate will put a mattock in his hands
And lash him while he digs himself the grave
That is to be the pallet and the shroud
Of his poor blundering bones."

Robinson gives a remarkably inclusive picture of Vivian and Merlin. Vivian is all concentration: her movement is centripetal. Her problem is her identification with Merlin here and now. Merlin represents the opposite: his movement is expansive, centrifugal. Yet he needs Vivian, and her concentrative force struggles against the wider obligation to Camelot—and indeed also against the promise he sees in the "Light" of the Grail. Merlin's mind is far-ranging, deeply contemplative and metaphysical. As he speaks with Dagonet the King's fool, Merlin goes far beyond the bounds of his own earthly needs to insist on

"an eternal will, strangely endowed
With merciful illusions whereby self
Becomes the will itself and each man swells
In fond accordance with his agency."

Merlin, who "saw too much," perceives the impending tragedy of Camelot; he sees, moreover, the permanance of that earthly passion which meant life and strength to him. With prophetic insight he speaks to Dagonet of Vivian.

"In time to be,
The like of her shall have another name
Than Vivian, and her laugh shall be a fire,
Not shining only to consume itself
With what it burns. She knows not yet the name
Of what she is, for now there is no name;
Some day there shall be."

In his moments of prophetic vision Merlin rises above the harshness of ordinary life. At these times he is an instrument of metaphysical truth far beyond conventional behavior or mere incantation. He knows "beyond knowledge," says Vivian. Here one finds a reminder of Merlin's far earlier and almost forgotten predecessors: the seer of Geoffrey's *Prophetiae Merlini* and Merlinus Silvestris of the *Vita Merlini*. In both of these works Merlin transcends the bounds of ordinary conduct in a wildly confusing series of disasters and predictions. In the *Prophetiae* the seer foretells "Woe to the perjured nation, for whose sake the renowned city [Winchester] shall come to ruin." With a flash of recognition we remember the scene in which Merlin and Dagonet talk of the doom of Camelot.

> The wizard shivered as he spoke, and stared
> Away into the sunset where he saw
> Once more, as through a cracked and cloudy glass,
> A crumbling sky that held a crimson cloud
> Wherein there was a town of many towers
> All swayed and shaken, in a woman's hand
> This time, till out of it there spilled and flashed
> And tumbled, like loose jewels, town, towers, and walls,
> And there was nothing but a crumbling sky
> That made anon of black and red and ruin
> A wild and final rain on Camelot.

In the *Vita Merlini* Myrddin, who goes mad after the death of his three brothers in battle, takes to the woods, and asks that a house be built with many windows, through which he can see the stars and discover what will happen to the kingdom. Like Robinson's Merlin, therefore, his remote ancestors see farther than ordinary men and are the prophets of great and often terrible events to come.

Merlin sees far because this is Robinson's way of looking at the world. It is a deeply penetrating view, unique in the history of the Arthurian legend. Robinson was determined, so far as possible, to get at the reality of experience. And for him reality was not simply the data of the senses: it was the totality of human perception. Readers have often been tempted to ponder the critical cliché: was Robinson a realist or a romanticist? Such Solomon's judgments are futile. If one thinks of dogmatic literary classifications one could say that he was both, like Melville and Thoreau and Conrad. Yet in a wider sense he is a realist. For him reality necessitated an expanded comprehension both of the world of sense and the world of idea, whereby he achieved a stereoscopic view of great depth and clarity.

In the more formal sense Robinson's awareness of reality makes him completely demythologize the legend. Merlin has no incantations that Vivian wishes to learn; the Holy Grail is not the sacred vessel of the sacrament but rather a kind of ethical guide, a "Light." It will be remembered that in like fashion Robinson completely eliminated the magic love-potion in his version of the Tristram story. His people are moderns: in all his poems they are easily recognizable as parts of our own experience.

A further dimension to Robinson's reality lies in an awareness of sensuous beauty not often found in his poetry. Broceliande is an earthly paradise in contrast with the gloom of Camelot. Merlin's arrival at Vivian's domain is described with delicate sensitivity.

> The birds were singing still; leaves flashed and swung
> Before him in the sunlight; a soft breeze
> Made intermittent whisperings around him
> Of love and fate and danger, and faint waves
> Of many sweetly-stinging fragile odors
> Broke lightly as they touched him; cherry boughs
> Above him snowed white petals down upon him,
> And under their slow falling Merlin smiled
> Contentedly, as one who contemplates
> No longer fear, confusion, or regret,
> May smile at ruin or at revelation.

Broceliande is indeed a very garden of pleasant delights for the embattled Merlin, and the beautiful Vivian is its mistress. Robinson describes her vividly.

> "More like a flower
> Tonight," he [Merlin] said, as now he scanned again
> The immemorial meaning of her face
> And drew it nearer to his eyes. It seemed
> A flower of wonder with a crimson stem
> Came leaning slowly and regretfully
> To meet his will—a flower of change and peril
> That had a clinging blossom of warm olive
> Half stifled with a tyranny of black,
> And held the wayward fragrance of a rose
> Made woman by delirious alchemy.

Merlin finds himself lapped in a world of luxurious sensation.

> Fatigue and hunger—tempered leisurely
> With food that some devout magician's oven
> Might after many failures have delivered,

And wine that had for decades in the dark
Of Merlin's grave been slowly quickening,
And with half-heard, dream-weaving interludes
Of distant flutes and viols, made more distant
By far, nostalgic hautboys blown from nowhere,—
Were tempered not so leisurely, may be,
With Vivian's inextinguishable eyes
Between two shining silver candlesticks
That lifted each a trembling flame to make
The rest of her a dusky loveliness
Against a bank of shadow.

In passages such as these Robinson explores another dimension of reality, the world of subtle sense impression and suggestion.

The truth of the imagination, capable of reaching into areas beyond the reach of logic, the acute awareness of the world of sense made animate by people who reason as well as feel—all these make *Merlin* a remarkably successful poem. It is not simply its originality which makes it likely to endure; Arthurian literature is filled with ill-conceived excursions off the beaten track of the legend. Apart from its originality, apart from a modern interpretation which strips the story of its old insistence on magic, Robinson has given us a poignant account of a doomed love, acted out by living people. The tragedy of the story of course is the impending fall of Camelot. No less moving, possibly even more so, is the pathos of Merlin's love for Vivian. It is an old story, but one that never loses its power. Merlin wrenches the heart in ways that Lancelot almost never does, for he has so much more to lose, psychologically, than Lancelot. To Merlin the experience of love was an unexpectedly demanding reversal. He who had been the prophetic sage, no expert in the ways of women, now had to become a lover. Lancelot always had been the servant of Venus. Yet the shattering emotional change Merlin undergoes never destroys his nobility, or the devotion of Vivian. They act out their loyalties and their disillusionments in a world which constantly suggests a dimension greater than Camelot.

IRVING HOWE

A Grave and Solitary Voice

The centennial of Edwin Arlington Robinson passed several years ago—he was born on December 22, 1869—with barely a murmur of public notice. There were a few academic volumes of varying merit, but no recognition in our larger journals and reviews, for Robinson seems the kind of poet who is likely to remain permanently out of fashion. At first, thinking about this neglect, I felt a surge of anger, since Robinson seems to me one of the best poets we have ever had in this country. But then, cooled by reflection and time, I came to see that perhaps it doesn't matter whether the writers we most care about receive their "due." Only the living need praise. Writers like Robinson survive in their work, appreciated by readers who aren't afraid to be left alone with an old book.

Robinson himself would hardly have expected any other fate, for he was not the sort of man to make demands on either this world or the next. Shy of all literary mobs, just managing to keep afloat through a workable mixture of Stoicism and alcohol, he lived entirely for his poetry. Most of the time he was very poor, and all of the time alone, a withdrawn and silent bachelor. He seems to have composed verse with that single-mindedness the rest of us keep for occasions of vanity and profit. As a result he wrote "too much," and his *Collected Poems,* coming almost to fifteen hundred crowded pages, has a great deal of failed work. But a small portion is very fine, and a group of fifteen or twenty poems unquestionably great.

This, to be sure, is not the received critical judgment—though a few critics, notably Conrad Aiken in some fine reviews of the 1920s and Yvor

From *The Critical Point: On Literature and Culture.* © 1973 by Irving Howe. Horizon Press, 1973.

Winters in a splendid little book published in 1946, have recognized his worth. The public acclaim of a Robert Frost, however, Robinson could never hope to match; the approval of the avant-garde, when it came at all, came in lukewarm portions, since T. S. Eliot had declared his work to be "negligible" and that, for a time, was that. Robinson stood apart from the cultural movements of his day, so much so that he didn't even bother to *oppose* literary modernism: he simply followed his own convictions. He was one of those New England solitaries—great-grandsons of the Puritans, nephews of the Emersonians—whose lives seem barren and pinched but who leave, in their stolid devotion to a task, something precious to the world.

The trouble in Robinson's life was mostly interior. Some force of repression, not exactly unknown to New England character, had locked up his powers for living by, or articulating openly, the feelings his poems show him to have had. Even in the poems themselves a direct release of passion or desire is infrequent; they "contain," or emerge out of, enormous depths of feeling, but it is a feeling pressed into oblique irony or disciplined into austere reflection. He was not the man to yield himself to what Henry James once called "promiscuous revelation."

Robinson lived mainly within himself, and sometimes near a group of admiring hangers-on who, as he seems to have known, were unworthy of him. Among his obsessive subjects are solitude and failure, both drawn from his immediate experience and treated with a richness of complication that is unequaled in American poetry. For the insights Robinson offered on these grim topics, in poems such as "The Wandering Jew" and "Eros Turannos," he no doubt paid a heavy price in his own experience. But we should remember that, finally, such preoccupations are neither a regional morbidity nor a personal neurosis: they are among the permanent and inescapable themes of literature. In his own dry and insular way, Robinson shared in the tragic vision that has dominated the imagination of the West since the Greek playwrights. By the time he began to write, it had perhaps become impossible for a serious poet to compose a tragedy on the classical scale, and as a result his sense of the tragic, unable to reach embodiment in a large action, had to emerge—one almost says, leak through—as a tone of voice, a restrained and melancholy contemplativeness.

At the age of twenty-two, Robinson could already write, half in wisdom and half in self-defense, sentences forming an epigraph to his whole career:

> Solitude . . . tends to magnify one's ideas of individuality; it
> sharpens his sympathy for failure where fate has been abused

and self demoralized; it renders a man suspicious of the whole natural plan, and leads him to wonder whether the invisible powers are a fortuitous issue of unguided cosmos.

Like Hawthorne and Melville before him, Robinson came from a family that had suffered both a fall in circumstances and a collapse of psychic confidence. To read the one reliable biography, by Herman Hagedorn, is gradually to be drawn into a graying orbit of family nightmare, an atmosphere painfully similar to that of a late O'Neill play. Tight-lipped quarrels, heavy drinking, failing investments, ventures into quack spiritualism and drugs—these were the matter of his youth. Hagedorn describes the few months before the death of the poet's father:

> [The elder Robinson's] interest in spiritualism had deepened and, in the slow disintegration of his organism, detached and eerie energies seemed to be released. There were table rappings and once the table came off the floor, "cutting my universe . . . clean in half." . . . Of these last months with his father, he told a friend, "They were a living hell."

Not much better were Robinson's early years in New York, where he slept in a hall bedroom and worked for a time as a subway clerk. He kept writing and won some recognition, including help from President Theodore Roosevelt, who was impressed by one of Robinson's (inferior) poems but had the honesty to admit he didn't understand it. Toward the end of his career Robinson scored his one commercial success with *Tristram*, the least interesting of his three lengthy Arthurian poems. This success did not much affect his life or, for that matter, his view of life. He died in 1935, a victim of cancer. It is said that as Robinson lay dying one of his hangers-on approached him for a small loan: life, as usual, trying to imitate art.

II

The imprint of New England on Robinson's sensibility is strong, but it is not precise. By the time he was growing up in the river-town of Gardiner, Maine (the Tilbury Town of his poems), Puritanism was no longer a coherent religious force. It had become at best a collective memory of moral rigor, an ingrained and hardened way of life surviving beyond its original moment of strength. Yet to writers like Hawthorne and Robinson, the New England tradition left a rich inheritance: the assumption that human existence, caught in a constant inner struggle between good and evil, is inherently dramatic; and the habit of intensive scrutiny, at once proud and dust-humble, into human motives, such as the old Puritans had used for discovering whether they were among the elect. Writers like Hawthorne and Robinson were no longer believers but since they still responded to what they had rejected, they found themselves in a fruitful dilemma. They did not wish entirely to shake off the inflexible moralism of the New England past; yet they were fascinated by the psychological study of behavior that would come to dominate twentieth-century literature and, meanwhile, was both a borrowing from nineteenth-century European romanticism and a distillation of Puritan habits of mind. The best of the New England writers tried to yoke these two ways of regarding the human enterprise, and if their attempt is dubious in principle, it yielded in practice a remarkable subtlety in the investigation of motives. As for Emersonianism, by the time Robinson was beginning to think for himself it was far gone in decay, barely discernible as specific doctrine and little more than a mist of genteel idealism.

Robinson borrowed from both traditions. His weaker poems reveal an Emersonian yearning toward godhead and transcendence, which is an experience somewhat different from believing in God. His stronger poems share with the Puritans a cast of mind that is intensely serious, convinced of the irreducibility of moral problems, and devoted to nuance of motive with the scrupulosity his grandfathers had applied to nuance of theology. Even in an early, unimpressive sonnet like "Credo," which begins in a dispirited tone characteristic of much late nineteenth-century writing,

> I cannot find my way: there is no star
> In all the shrouded heavens anywhere

Robinson still felt obliged to end with an Emersonian piety:

> I know the far-sent message of the years,
> I feel the coming glory of the Light.

Whenever that "Light" begins to flicker, so tenuous a symbol for the idea of transcendence, it is a sure sign of trouble in Robinson's poems. A straining toward an optimism in which he has no real conviction, it would soon be overshadowed, however, by Robinson's darkening fear, as he later wrote in a long poem called *King Jasper,* that

> No God,
> No Law, no Purpose, could have hatched for sport
> Out of warm water and slime, a war for life
> That was unnecessary, and far better

Never had been—if man, as we behold him,
Is all it means.

Such lines suggest that Robinson's gift was not for strict philosophizing in verse; he was eminently capable of thinking as a poet, but mainly through his arrangement of dramatic particulars and the casual reflections he wove in among them. What makes Robinson's concern with God and the cosmos important is not its doctrinal content, quite as vague in statement and dispirited in tone as that of other sensitive people of his time, but the way in which he would employ it as the groundwork for his miniature dramas. Fairly conventional doctrine thereby becomes the living tissue of suffering and doubt.

It is an advantage for a writer to have come into relation with a great tradition of thought, even if only in its stages of decay, and it can be a still greater advantage to struggle with the problem of salvaging elements of wisdom from that decayed tradition. For while a culture in decomposition may limit the scope of its writers and keep them from the highest achievement, it offers special opportunities for moral drama to those who can maintain their bearing. The traps of such a moment are obvious: nostalgia, on the one extreme, and sensationalism, on the other. Most of the time Robinson was strong enough to resist these temptations, a portion of the old New England steel persisting in his soul; or perhaps he could resist them simply because he was so entirely absorbed in his own sense of the human situation and therefore didn't even trouble about the cultural innovations and discoveries of his time. He made doubt into a discipline, and failure into an opening toward compassion. The old principles of his culture may have crumbled, but he found his subject in the problems experienced by those to whom the allure of those principles had never quite dulled.

III

Many of Robinson's shorter poems—lyrics, ballads, sonnets, dramatic narratives—are set in Tilbury Town, his Down East locale where idlers dream away their lives in harmless fantasy, mild rebels suffer the resistance of a community gone stiff, and the tragedy of personal isolation seems to acquire a universal character, as if speaking for Robinson's vision of America, perhaps all of life. Other nineteenth-century writers had of course employed a recurrent setting in their work, and later Faulkner would do the same with Yoknapatawpha County. Yet Robinson's use of Tilbury Town is rather different from what these writers do: he makes no attempt to fill out its social world, he cares little about details of place and moment, he seems hardly to strive for historical depth. Tilbury Town is more an atmosphere than a setting, it is barely drawn or provisioned, and it serves to suggest less a vigorous community than a felt lack of historical continuity. The foreground figures in these poems are drawn with two or three harsh, synoptic strokes, but Tilbury Town itself is shadowy, fading into the past and no longer able to bind its people. Robinson eyes it obliquely, half in and half out of its boundaries, a secret sharer taking snapshots of decline. To illuminate a world through a glimpsed moment of crisis isn't, for him, a mere strategy of composition; it signifies his deepest moral stance, a nervous signature of reticence and respect. He seems always to be signaling a persuasion that nothing can be known with certainty and the very thought of direct assertion is a falsehood in the making.

Some of these Tilbury pieces, as Robinson once remarked, have been "pickled in anthological brine." Almost "everybody" knows "Miniver Cheevy" and "Richard Cory," sardonic vignettes of small-town character, Yankee drop-outs whose pitiable condition is contrasted—in quirky lines and comic rhymes—with their weak fantasies. These are far from Robinson's best poems, but neither are they contemptible. In the sketch of poor Miniver, who "loved the days of old," there are flashes of cleverness:

> Miniver mourned the ripe renown
>   That made so many a name so fragrant;
> He mourned Romance, now on the town,
>   And Art, a vagrant.

Such pieces lead to better ones of their kind, such as the tautly written sonnets about Reuben Bright, the butcher who tears down his slaughterhouse when told his wife must die, and Aaron Stark, a miser with "eyes like little dollars in the dark." My experience in teaching these poems is that students trained to flounder in *The Waste Land* will at first condescend, but when asked to read the poems again, will be unsettled by the depths of moral understanding Robinson has hidden away within them.

The finest of Robinson's sonnets of character is "The Clerks." Describing a return to Tilbury Town, the poet meets old friends, figures of "a shopworn brotherhood," who now work as clerks in stores. The opening octet quietly evokes this scene, and then in the closing sestet Robinson widens the range of his observation with a powerful statement about the weariness of slow defeat:

> And you that ache so much to be sublime,
> And you that feed yourselves with your descent,

> What comes of all your visions and your fears?
> Poets and kings are but the clerks of Time,
> Tiering the same dull webs of discontent,
> Clipping the same sad alnage of the years.

Without pretending to close analysis, I would like to glance at a few of the perceptual and verbal refinements in these six lines. The opening "ache . . . to be sublime" has its workaday irony that prepares for the remarkable line which follows: to "feed" with "your descent" is a characteristic Robinsonian turn, which in addition to the idea of consuming oneself through age suggests more obliquely that indulgence in vanity which claims distinction for one's decline. Poets and kings who are "clerks of Time" are helplessly aligned with the Tilbury clerks, yet Robinson sees that even in the democracy of our common decay we cling to our trifle of status. For in the "dull webs of discontent" which form the fragile substance of our lives, we still insist on "tiering" ourselves. Coming in the penultimate line, the word "tiering" has enormous ironic thrust: how long can a tier survive as a web? And then in the concluding line Robinson ventures one of his few deviations from standard English, in the use of "alnage," a rare term meaning a measure of cloth, that is both appropriate to the atmosphere of waste built up at the end and overwhelming as it turns us back to the "shop-worn" clerks who are Robinson's original donnée.

Now, for readers brought up in the modernist tradition of Eliot and Stevens, these short poems of Robinson will not yield much excitement. They see in such poems neither tangle nor agony, brilliance nor innovation. But they are wrong, for the Tilbury sonnets and lyrics do, in their own way, represent a significant innovation: Robinson was the first American poet of stature to bring commonplace people and commonplace experience into our poetry. Whitman had invoked such people and even rhapsodized over them, but as individual creatures with warm blood they are not really to be found in his pages. Robinson understood that

> Even the happy morals we term ordinary or commonplace act
> their own mental tragedies and live a far deeper and wider life
> than we are inclined to believe possible.

The point bears stressing because most critics hail poets like Eliot and Stevens for their innovations in metrics and language while condescending toward Robinson as merely traditional. Even if that were true, it would not, of course, be a sufficient reason for judgments either favorable or hostile; but it is not true. Robinson never thought of himself as a poetic revolutionary, but like all major poets he helped enlarge for those who came after him the possibilities of composition. The work of gifted writers like Robert Lowell, James Dickey, and James Wright was enabled by Robinson's muted innovations.

His dramatic miniatures in verse—spiritual dossiers of American experience, as someone has nicely called them—remind one a little of Hawthorne, in their ironic undercurrents and cool explorations of vanity, and a little of James, in their peeling away of psychic pretense and their bias that human relationships are inherently a trap. Yet it would be unjust to say that Robinson was a short-story writer who happened to write verse, for it is precisely through the traditional forms he employed—precisely through his disciplined stanzas, regular meters, and obbligatos of rhyme—that he released his vision. Robinson's language seldom achieves the high radiance of Frost, and few of his short poems are as beautifully complexioned as Frost's "Spring Pools" or "The Most of It." But in Robinson there are sudden plunges into depths of experiences, and then stretches of earned contemplativeness, that Frost can rarely equal. Here, for example, is the octet of a Robinson sonnet, "The Pity of the Leaves," that deals with an experience—an old man alone at night with his foreboding of death—which in "An Old Man's Winter Night" Frost also treated memorably but not, I think, as well:

> Vengeful across the cold November moors,
> Loud with ancestral shame there came the bleak
> Sad wind that shrieked and answered with a shriek,
> Reverberant through lonely corridors.
> The old man heard it; and he heard, perforce,
> Words out of lips that were no more to speak—
> Words of the past that shook the old man's cheek
> Like dead remembered footsteps on old floors.

It is always to "the slow tragedy of haunted men" that Robinson keeps returning. One of his greatest lyrics on this theme, the kind of hypnotic incantation that *happens* to a poet once or twice if he is lucky, is "Luke Havergal": a grieving man hears the voice of his dead love and it draws him like an appetite for death, a beauty of death quiet and enclosing.

The greatest of these Tilbury poems, and one of the greatest poems about the tragedy of love in our language, is "Eros Turannos." Yvor Winters aptly calls it "a universal tragedy in a Maine setting." It deals with a genteel and sensitive woman, advancing in years and never, apparently, a startling beauty, who has married or otherwise engaged herself to a charming wastrel with a taste for the finer things of life:

> She fears him, and will always ask
>   What fated her to choose him;
> She meets in his engaging mask
>   All reasons to refuse him.

With a fierce concentration of phrase, the poem proceeds to specify the entanglements in which these people trap themselves, the moral confusions and psychic fears, all shown with a rare balance of exactness and compassion. The concluding stanza reaches a wisdom about the human lot such as marks Robinson's poetry at its best. Those, he writes, who with the god of love have striven,

> Not hearing much of what we say,
>   Take what the god has given;
> Though like waves breaking it may be,
> Or like a changed familiar tree,
> Or like a stairway to the sea
>   Where down the blind are driven.

Thinking of such poems and trying to understand how it is that in their plainness they can yet seem so magnificent, one finds oneself falling back on terms like "sincerity" and "honesty." They are terms notoriously inadequate and tricky, yet inescapable in discussing poets like Robinson and Thomas Hardy. It is not, after all, as if one wants to say about more brilliant poets like Eliot and Yeats that they are insincere or lacking in honesty; of course not. What one does want to suggest is that in poems like Robinson's "Eros Turannos" and "Hillcrest," as in Hardy's "The Going" and "At Castle Boterel," there is an abandonment of all pretense and pose, all protectiveness and persona. At such moments the poet seems beyond decoration and defense; he leaves himself vulnerable, open to the pain of his self; he cares nothing for consolation; he looks at defeat and does not blink. It is literature beyond the literary.

IV

Robinson was also a master of a certain genre poem, Wordsworthian in tone and perhaps source, which Frost also wrote but not, in my judgment, as well. These are poems about lost and aging country people, mostly in New England: "Isaac and Archibald," "Aunt Imogen," and "The Poor Relation." The very titles are likely to displease readers whose hearts tremble before titles like "Leda and the Swan," "The Idea of Order at Key West," and "The Bridge." A pity!

"Isaac and Archibald" is the masterpiece of this group, a summer idyll tinged with shadows of death, told by a mature man remembering himself as a boy who spent an afternoon with two old farmers, lifelong friends, each of whom now frets that the other is showing signs of decay. The verse is exquisite:

> So I lay dreaming of what things I would,
> Calm and incorrigibly satisfied
> With apples and romance and ignorance,
> And the still smoke from Archibald's clay pipe.
> There was a stillness over everything,
> As if the spirit of heat had laid its hand
> Upon the world and hushed it; and I felt
> Within the mightiness of the white sun
> That smote the land around us and wrought out
> A fragrance from the trees, a vital warmth
> And fulness for the time that was to come,
> And a glory for the world beyond the forest.
> The present and the future and the past,
> Isaac and Archibald, the burning bush,
> The Trojans and the walls of Jericho,
> Were beautifully fused; and all went well
> Till Archibald began to fret for Isaac
> And said it was a master day for sunstroke.

Another kind of poem at which Robinson showed his mastery, one that has rarely been written in this country, is the dramatic monologue of medium length. "Rembrandt to Rembrandt," "The Three Taverns" (St. Paul approaching Rome), and "John Brown" are the best examples. The pitfalls of this genre are notorious: an effort to capture the historic inflections of the speaker's voice, so that both conciseness of speech and poetic force are sacrificed to some idea of verisimilitude; a tendency toward linguistic exhibitionism, blank verse as a mode of preening; and a lack of clear focusing of intent, so that the immediate experience of the speaker fails to take on larger resonance. Robinson mostly transcends these difficulties. He chooses figures at moments of high crisis, Rembrandt as he plunges into his dark painting, St. Paul as he ruminates upon his forthcoming capture, and John Brown as he readies himself for hanging. The result is serious in moral perception, leading always to the idea of abandonment of the self, and dignified in tone, for Robinson had little gift for colloquial speech and was shrewd enough to maintain a level of formal diction.

It is Frost who is mainly honored for this kind of dramatic poem, but a sustained comparison would show, I think, the superiority of Robinson's work. Though not nearly so brilliant a virtuoso as Frost, Robinson writes from a fullness of experience and a tragic awareness that Frost cannot equal. Frost has a strong grasp on the melodramatic extremes of behavior, but he lacks almost entirely Robinson's command of its middle ranges. Frost achieves a cleaner verbal surface, but Robinson is more abundant in moral detail and insight.

There remains finally a word to be said about Robinson's Arthurian poems, *Merlin, Lancelot,* and *Tristram,* the first two of which are very considerable productions. I am aware of straining my readers' credulity in saying that *Merlin* and *Lancelot,* set in the court of King Arthur and dealing with the loves and intrigues of his knights, are profound explorations of human suffering.

Tennyson's *Idylls of the Kings,* dealing with the same materials, is mainly a pictorial representation of waxen figures, beautiful in the way a tapestry might be but not very gripping as drama. Robinson's Guinevere and Lancelot, however, are errant human beings separated from us only by costume and time; his Merlin is an aging man of worldly power and some wisdom who finds himself drawn to the temptations of private life. Long poems are bound to have flaws, in this case excessive talk and a spun-thin moral theorizing that can become tedious. There is the further problem that any effort at sustained blank verse will, by now, lead to padding and looseness of language. Still, these are poems for mature men and women who know that in the end we are all as we are, vulnerable and mortal. Here Merlin speaks at the end of his career, remembering his love:

> Let her love
> What man she may, no other love than mine
> Shall be an index of her memories.
> I fear no man who may come after me,
> And I see none. I see her, still in green,
> Beside the fountain. I shall not go back.
>
> . . . .
> If I come not,
> The lady Vivian will remember me,
> And say: "I knew him when his heart was young.
> Though I have lost him now. Time called him home,
> And that was as it was; for much is lost
> Between Broceliande and Camelot."

In my own experience Robinson is a poet who grows through rereading, or perhaps it would be better to say, one grows into being able to reread
him. He will never please the crowds, neither the large ones panting for
platitude nor the small ones supposing paradox an escape from platitude.
All that need finally be said about Robinson he said himself in a sonnet
about George Crabbe, the eighteenth-century English poet who also wrote
about commonplace people in obscure corners of the earth:

> Whether or not we read him, we can feel
> From time to time the vigor of his name
> Against us like a finger for the shame
> And emptiness of what our souls reveal
> In books that are as altars where we kneel
> To consecrate the flicker, not the flame.

JOSEPHINE MILES

Robinson and the Years Ahead

The title of Edwin Arlington Robinson's early book, *The Children of the Night,* suggests its place in romantic tradition and its participation in the poetics of the 1890s, the poetics of starlight, dream, and death. The first poem begins:

> "Where are you going to-night, to-night,—
>   Where are you going, John Evereldown?
> There's never the sign of a star in sight,
>   Nor a lamp that's nearer than Tilbury Town.
> Why do you stare as a dead man might?
> Where are you pointing away from the light?
> And where are you going to-night, to-night,—
>   Where are you going, John Evereldown?"

Much of his poetry is in these lines—the strong formal use of repetition, the tone of conversation, the ballad-like mysteries and assumptions, the language of dreary atmosphere. Robinson's contemporaries in British poetry were Swinburne, Hardy, Housman, Wilde, Yeats; after Dickinson, in American, Sill, Lanier, Guiney, Moody, Sterling, Frost. He is clearly of their number in the tradition of major vocabulary of *good, god, man, time, world, make, see,* and in the romanticisms from the earlier world of Coleridge which supply at least a third of his chief substance.

It was Coleridge above all who turned away from the acceptances of the eighteenth century, away from these even in his own poetry, toward a

From *Poetry and Change.* © 1974 by the Regents of the University of California. University of California Press, 1974.

new implicativeness of inner searching. Often when such a turn is made, it is made in terms of a familiar old antique material. As the young Chatterton purportedly experimented in the recovering of old styles and seemed new in his uses, which were actually close to the classical narrations of his predecessor Waller, so Robinson was taken as notably new for his day, while he retold again the Arthurian stories which Tennyson had told before. As Coleridge's monody recalled,

> And we, at sober eve, would round thee throng,
> Hanging, enraptured, on thy stately song;
> And greet with smiles the young-eyed *Poesy*
> All deftly masked, as hoar *Antiquity.*

The young-eyed poesy was the poesy of noble narrative for Chatterton. Whether ballad-like or satiric, it was commonly martial, and it dealt with great virtues and passions.

> O Chryste, it is a grief for me to telle,
> How manie a nobil erle and valrous knyghte
> In fyghtynge for Kynge Harrold noblie fell,
> Al sleyne in Hastyngs feeld in bloudie fyghte,
> O sea! our teeming donore han thy floude,
> Han anie fructous entendement,
> Thou wouldst have rose and sank wyth tydes of bloude,
> Before Duke Wyllam's knyghts han hither went;
>   Whose cowart arrows manie erles sleyne,
>   And brued the feeld wyth bloude as season rayne.
>
> And of his knyghtes did eke full manie die,
> All passyng hie, of mickle myghte echone,
> Whose poygnant arrowes, typp'd with destynie,
> Caus'd manie wydowes to make myckle mone.
> Lordynges, avaunt, that chycken-harted are,
> Frrom out of hearynge quicklie now departe;
> Full well I wote, to synge of bloudie warre
> Will greeve your tenderlie and mayden harte.
>   Go, do the weaklie womman inn mann's geare,
>   And scond your mansion if grymm war come there.

This beginning of his "Battle of Hastings," characteristic of his work as a whole, takes the view of a narrator; he *tells,* he *sings,* of those heroes who *rise, stand, seek, fly, fall, die.* The persons are *kings, knights, earls,* classical *friends,* and, as in the ballads, *fathers* and *sons;* the scene is *ground* and *plain,* the tools are *spears* and *arrows,* thus antique; the results, *wounds, blood, woe.* For all these, the chief value terms are in keeping, the relatively rare *bloody, brave, dead,* the rarer *mickle,* and then the neoclassical *good, great, high, noble, sweet* of Edmund Waller exactly, and in part of Denham, Joseph Warton, Creech, Fairfax, that is, of the classical narrative tradition in English.

The Wartons and others who argued the dating of the Rowley poems recognized "in point of style, composition, and sentiment" the very traits which this vocabulary represents: the ideal and abstract terms, compound epithets, smoothness of meter, "all that elegance, firmness of contexture, srength and brilliancy, which did not appear in our poetry before the middle of the present century." True, the central neoclassical mode; but its early name was Waller; it was held in check, away from the Gothic sublime extremes of the Wartons, by the pull of the narrative, even the ballad narrative, tradition.

Percy's *Ballads* were not folk ballads in structure, because they smoothed the lines to a classical norm, filled in with adjectives and sentiments, and generally did to "Chevy Chase" what Pope did to Donne, or what her family did to Emily Dickinson: tidied up the implications and made both beat and sentiment regularly explicit. Given the steadiness of frame and feeling, the eighteenth-century "firmness of contexture," Chatterton was able to work in the opposite direction, to irregularize intermittently, by means of a lively action and a mixed vocabulary, the smooth neoclassic conventions of narrative in his time. In Waller, the pose of this tradition, the first of "Love's Farewell,"

> Treading the path to noble ends,
> A long farewell to love I gave,
> Resolved my country, and my friends,
> All that remain'd of me should have.

Like Waller, Chatterton explored a variety, straight and satiric narrative, pastoral, a kind of ballad tradition; the very curious mixture of conventions which we see in his vocabulary provided a neoclassic basis for romance. "He fell in love," his mother said, "with the illuminated capitals of an old musical manuscript in French." The mickel illuminations of antiquity, of romance, graced Chatterton's text on its surface and in its spirit of Miniver Cheevy with which Robinson sympathized.

Those most conscious of moving ahead are most deeply involved in the past. As Chatterton cast an atmosphere forward, so did Robinson. Robinson shared his atmosphere with a few poetic allies and set his name upon it for the future. His especially are the adjectives of *desolate, human, lonely, lost, sad,* the nouns of *faith, flame, gleam, glory, shame, truth, thought, touch, hell, music, song, woman, wisdom, wall;* the verbs of *call* and *feel,* the chief connectives characteristically few except for the relative *that.* The atmosphere, the yearning, the generalizing of human values in inner hope and shame:

> Go to the western gate, Luke Havergal,
> There where the vines cling crimson on the wall,
> . . . .
> But go, and if you listen she will call.
>
> . . . .
> No, there is not a dawn in eastern skies
> To rift the fiery night that's in your eyes;
>
> . . . .
> God slays Himself with every leaf that flies,
> And hell is more than half of paradise.
>
> . . . .
> Nor think to riddle the dead words they say,
> Nor any more to feel them as they fall.

So the lines of every poem are loaded and reloaded with the terms of value. From "Three Quatrains," for example, the music, with abstraction: "As long as Fame's imperious music rings." From "Dear Friends" too:

> So, friends (dear friends), remember, if you will,
> The shame I win for singing is all mine,
> The gold I miss for dreaming is all yours.

From "The Story of the Ashes and the Flame," the emotional strains of "The story was as old as human shame." From "Zola":

> Because he puts the compromising chart
> Of hell before your eyes, you are afraid;
> . . . .
> Never until we conquer the uncouth
> Connivings of our shamed indifference
> (We call it Christian faith) are we to scan
> The racked and shrieking hideousness of Truth.

From "The Pity of the Leaves": "Loud with ancestral shame there came the bleak / Sad wind." From "Cliff Klingenhagen": "And when I asked him . . . he only looked at me / And smiled." The whole thought of "The Dead Village" and of "Credo"—the ghost of things—and, from "Verlaine," "Song sloughs away the sin to find redress / In art's complete remembrance." From "Supremacy," the measures of "There is a drear and lonely tract of hell." And the full array of "Octaves":

> We thrill too strangely at the master's touch;
> We shrink too sadly from the larger self
>
> . . . .
>
> We dare not feel it yet—the splendid shame
> Of uncreated failure; we forget,
> The while we groan, that God's accomplishment
> Is always and unfailingly at hand.

And:

> With conscious eyes not yet sincere enough
> To pierce the glimmered cloud that fluctuates
> Between me and the glorifying light
> That screens itself with knowledge, I discern
> The searching rays of wisdom that reach through
> The mist of shame's infirm credulity,
> And infinitely wonder if hard words
> Like mine have any message for the dead.

And "L'Envoi":

> Now in a thought, now in a shadowed word,
> Now in a voice that thrills eternity,
> Ever there comes an onward phrase to me
> Of some transcendent music I have heard;
> No piteous thing by soft hands dulcimered,
> No trumpet crash of blood-sick victory,
> But a glad strain of some vast harmony
> That no brief mortal touch has ever stirred.
> There is no music in the world like this,
> No character wherewith to set it down,
> No kind of instrument to make it sing.
> No kind of instrument? Ah, yes, there is;

> And after time and place are overthrown,
> God's touch will keep its one chord quivering.

These are the poems of the nineties, of Robinson's first work. Thirty years later, in *Avon's Harvest* and other poems, and in his most famous *Tristram,* in culmination of the Arthur sequence, the same characteristic phrasings prevail.

> Fear, like a living fire that only death
> Might one day cool, had now in Avon's eyes
> Been witness . . .
> He smiled, but I would rather he had not
>
> . . . .
>   I was awake for hours,
> Toiling in vain to let myself believe
> That Avon's apparition was a dream.

Steadily the insistence is on the mystery, interiority, often horror, sometimes majesty, of human feelings scarcely formulable—the "old human swamps" of Avon, the phantom sound of Roland's horn for Mr. Flood—the vividly implicative narrative turning inward so characteristic of the English nineteenth century in Coleridge, Browning, Yeats. "Modernities" is a fine and explicitly commentary example in concentration. *Tristram* takes up the same ground in a more leisurely way: *Isolt of the white hands . . . white birds . . . remembered . . . her father . . . smiling in the way she feared . . . Throbbing as if she were a child . . . For making always of a distant wish / A dim belief . . . How many scarred cold things that once had laughed . . . a cold soul-retching wave . . . And body and soul were quick to think of it . . . Smiling as one who suffers to escape / Through silence and familiar misery, . . . Lost in a gulf of time where time was lost—and at the end—He smiled like one with nothing else to do; . . . It was like that / For women sometimes, . . . Alone, with her white face and her gray eyes, / She watched them there till even her thoughts were white, . . . And the white sunlight flashing on the sea.*

The terms in which the later poems differ from the earlier are mostly terms required by the content: for example, the *father, king,* and *queen, forget, remember,* and *wait* of Isolt's life in the Tristram story. Some of the differences are, however, more significant of attitude. Later *sick* takes the place of earlier *dead;* sensory *cold* and *white,* the place of more commentary *desolate, lonely, sad.* Similarly, objective nouns *bird, fire, moon, shadow* take the place of more commentary *gleam, glory, faith, shame.* The musical references fade. The ironies of *laugh* and *smile* are heightened. In other words, objectivities do more of the work in the later verse; it is the same work, cooled.

> We saw that fire at work within his eyes
> And had no glimpse of what was burning there. . . .
> . . . and there was now
> No laughing in that house. . . .
> . . . without the sickening weight of added years.
> . . . a made smile of acquiescence, . . .
> . . . he who sickens . . . over the fire of sacrifice . . .
> He smiled, but I would rather he had not.

These lines and many more in their vein from *Avon;* and, from "Rembrandt," "shadows and obscurities":

> "Touching the cold offense of my decline,"
> . . . like sick fruit . . . our stricken souls . . .
> Your soul may laugh . . . or grinning evil
> In a golden shadow . . .
> Forget your darkness in the dark, and hear
> No longer the cold wash of Holland scorn.
> The moon that glimmered cold on Brittany . . .
> How many scarred cold things that once had laughed
> And loved, and wept, and sung, and had been men, . . .
> . . . a cold soul-retching wave
> . . . And body and soul were sick to think of it.
> . . . White birds . . . Before his eyes were blinded by white
>   irons . . .
>   And when slow rain
> Fell cold upon him as upon hot fuel,
> It might as well have been a rain of oil
> On faggots round some creature at a stake
> For all the quenching there was in it then
> Of a sick sweeping beast consuming him
> With anguish of intolerable loss.
> . . . The still white fire of her necessity.

With these backward looks of his, Robinson also looked forward. If not an innovator, he was at least an early participant in new and future developments. While with Frost he was one of the last to stress thought and thinking, his feeling, telling, singing, song, and music he shared with his contemporary William Vaughn Moody, with Chivers and Sterling, and then with Wallace Stevens. His verb of *touch* he shared with Sill and Swinburne; his *human,* with Sterling and Stevens; his *face* and *nothing* with Poe and Stevens. Then, especially with the young modern poets of mid-twentieth century, his romantic *cold, small, white, bird, fire, flame, dream, shadow,* and his especial *sick.*

Writers on Robinson have agreed with Redman, one of the earliest, that his first books revealed the method and matter of his maturity and that his New England childhood, Harvard education, New York and McDowell work and writing, all kept him to "the seasons and the sunset as before." He was no explorer or revolutionary. He saw each man trying to cope with his own demon, as in "Rembrandt," and each a child "trying to spell *God* with wrong blocks." So he saw experience and expectation often at odds, and so his characteristic early vocabulary gives us the heart of his poetry with its blend of sense and sensibility—*touch, sing, shine, flame, gleam,* with *desolate, lonely, human, shame, wisdom, truth,* while *Avon* and *Tristram* add *cold, sick, white, shadow, smile, remember* to *nothing* and *time.* This was a world already established by Coleridge and Poe, and enforced by Robinson's own contemporaries, yet in a way he was right that he looked forward, because much of his terminology has been strengthened by the poets of the mid-twentieth century. Sill's *small, still, touch, watch,* Sterling's *vision* and *gleam,* Moody's *low, sick, road,* Stevens's *large, human, music,* Williams's *flame, call, seek,* W. T. Scott's *memory* and *remember,* Hecht's *cold,* move into Rothenberg's *lost, hell, grow, leave,* much *white* and *shadow,* the *cold* of Snyder and others, Ray's *woman,* Kelly's *music* and *song,* and McClure's *sick, dream, flame, memory, nothing, wall, remember, touch*—the connotative, implicative, nostalgic sense of beauty in the world today. Esther Willard Bates reported, in *Edwin Arlington Robinson and His Manuscripts,* "He told me that he was, perhaps, two hundred years in advance of his time, indicating in brief half-statements, with pauses in between, that his habit of understatement, his absorption in the unconscious and semi conscious feelings and impulses of his characters were the qualities in which he was unlike his contemporaries. . . . He said he wondered if he wasn't too dry, too plain, if he wasn't overdoing the simple, the unpoetic phrase."

Yet this was the poet who "knew his Bible" and who was quoted by his biographer Hagedorn as characteristically writing, "In the great shuffle of transmitted characteristics, traits, abilities, aptitudes, the man who fixes on something definite in life that he must do, at the expense of everything else, if necessary, has presumably got something that, for him, should be recognized as the Inner Fire. For him, that is the Gleam, the Vision, and the Word! He'd better follow it."

What have the Gleam, the Vision, and the Word got to do with understatement dry, plain, and unpoetic? How does Robinson reconcile objects of nature with concepts of desire, Tennyson's atmospheres with Browning's interior psychologizing, rich sense with metaphysical thought so that he seems at once modern and out of date, at once reminiscent and inventive? His major vocabulary provides one suggestion toward an answer: that his chief material is romantic natural beauty, but that his treatment of it is skeptical, unhappy, in a metaphysics of *shame, lonely,* and *sick.* Such a tone preserves him his modernity through a moonlit world. *Desolate, human, shame, truth, wisdom* are the terms of interpretive comment which his critics call literary, and which distinguish him from metaphysicians like Frost, on the one hand, and in their negativity from the American poets of praise like Whitman, on the other hand. He praises with nostalgia and he blames with apprehension; many young poets today share this combination of attitudes and even this vocabulary of values. To see more vividly how little "metaphysical" was his tradition, we may look again at Donne, to see what we have lost and what we have gained.

.

JOHN LUCAS

The Poetry
of Edwin Arlington Robinson

When Edwin Arlington Robinson died in 1935, his loss was mourned
not only by America's writers but by statesmen and citizens whom one
would not readily accuse of an interest in literature. Robinson was a famous
man. Now, some thirty years later, the fame has shrunk, and it is my guess
that the works are very little read. Certainly it is a matter of some difficulty
to find a copy of his collected works. Not that Robinson has been neglected
by literary historians or wiped from the record of American poetry. Far
from it; his position has never been more secure. But that is just the trouble.
Talking recently with some American undergraduates about modern American poetry, I asked them why it was that Robinson was so little read now-
adays. "Well, you see," one of them explained, "we know just about where
he stands." The implication was that once you had got your author firmly
placed, any need to read his works had more or less disappeared. It was an
unnerving instance of what can happen to the ideal of discrimination, and
even more of what literary history frequently comes to mean to students of
literature. It seems to me worth the effort, therefore, to try to unsettle some
of the suavely held convictions about Robinson, not so much in the interest
of quarrelling with his standing as to suggest that, whatever that may be, he
is a poet whose best work deserves to be kept alive.

But where does Robinson stand? Not very high, to be sure. He comes
a long way below Frost, for example, though some way above Jeffers, and
it is easy enough to put him in his place. A gesture in the direction of "Luke
Havergal," mention of "The Man against the Sky," a word of judicious

From *Moderns and Contemporaries*. © 1985 by John Lucas. Barnes & Noble
Books, 1985.

praise for "Eros Turannos," and that is more or less that. If more is said, it likely enough consists of making out a table of faults. And since these are obvious, there is no great problem about setting them down. Robinson wrote too much; he fashioned too many long narrative poems out of too little material; his plays are uniformly dull; at times he falls into a ponderous prosiness of style, especially in his later years; his regard for the trivial is often trivial. But I think that the faults can be cheerfully admitted because they do not harm the virtues. When we have done with listing all Robinson's vices and pointing to the pages that can be skipped, there still remains a sizeable body of work that anyone who cares about poetry should want to read and reread. There is also, I have found, work that you prepare to skip and then forget to. For Robinson has the ability to write the plainest of plain tales in which his fascination with the quotidian of life becomes so remarkable that you find yourself either compelled to share it or to speculate on the manner of mind that could retain such open-eyed awe before the trivial.

This awe is an essential part of his vision. It is how he chooses to see and record his America. As is well known, Robinson's America is small-town New England, and he is the most distinguished product of a generation of writers that was rediscovering a need to voice a consciousness of being American. Now that this need has been written into the literary histories it seems obvious enough, but at the time itself it came as a revolutionary impulse. For the story of American poetry at the end of the nineteenth century is largely one of gentle, drab imitative work versus new and for the most part unrecognised efforts to cope with the American experience. The imitators looked East for their models; they hoped for nothing more than to come in a discreet second-best to Europe's literature, and predictably enough their work was highly praised. As late as 1915, for example, Fred Pattee, in *A History of American Literature since 1870,* was full of kind words for Celia Thaxter, Richard Hovey, Richard Watson Gilder and Emma Lazarus, among others, while completely ignoring Robinson, and this though much of Robinson's best work had by then been published. True, Pattee thought Emily Dickinson's poems should have been buried with her—"to compare her eccentric fragments with Blake's elfin wildness is ridiculous." But this merely provides further proof of how representative he is of what American critics wanted from their poets.

Yet the odd and, in a way, heartening thing is, that several of the poets Pattee so admired had an inkling that their deferential attitude to the old world wouldn't really do. One of them, Emma Lazarus, spoke out on behalf of a native American poetic:

> How long, and yet how long
> Our leaders will we hail from over seas,
> Masters and kings from feudal monarchies,
>   And mock their ancient song
> With echoes weak of foreign melodies?

But as that stanza makes very clear, she herself had to sing in decidedly weak echoes of foreign melodies. Although she has the good sense to realise that:

> The echo faints and fails;
> It suiteth not, upon this western plain,
> Our voice or spirit

Her own voice never emerges from the borrowed language of nineteenth-century English poetry. Before 1890 the only alternative to this appeared to lie in the verse of journalists like Ben King, Eugene Field and James Whit-comb Riley, whose work amounts to the homespun wisdom of old codgers tricked out in the various dialects of the middle west. *The Leaves of Grass,* it seems, was not an example to be followed.

The first, hesitant steps in breaking away from this appalling inheritance of native hayseed and imported Pre-Raphaelitism were taken in the verse of William Vaughn Moody and Trumbull Stickney. (I leave out of account Stephen Crane who, though certainly a remarkable talent, was too isolated and exceptional a case to be of any use to his contemporaries.) Here at last was an attempt to write serious verse that could cut free of tepid imitation. Stickney and Moody were Harvard poets, and a certain academicism shows in their verse; they are a little too eager to impose their sense of a classical philosophy on American observations; they dislike much of what they have to record but trust to a well-trained mind and a tasteful Stoicism to see them through the worst. Neither is a considerable poet, though Stickney might have become one had he lived, and Moody has some commendable passages. (I take it that one of his better poems, "Ode in Time of Hesitation," is a starting point for Lowell's "For the Union Dead.")

But more important than their poetic achievements was the climate for poetry that Moody and Stickney did so much to create during their Harvard years. They edited the Harvard *Monthly,* which under them won an enviable reputation as a magazine of high literary standards, and they set about looking for young contemporaries who could help them achieve the renaissance of American poetry. Curiously, however, they overlooked Robinson. Robinson entered Harvard in 1891, and he soon began publishing verse in the *Advocate*. But he never made the pages of the *Monthly*. Why this should be is difficult to say, for he was by far the most gifted of the Harvard poets, and by rights he ought to have been exactly the poet Moody and Stickney were looking for. But his personal situation may account for much. In his study of the *American 1890s*, Larzer Ziff points out that Robinson "was somewhat older than the average freshman, he was not a regular student, he came with academic deficiencies, and he had no social connections." These are bulky obstacles, and they may be enough to explain why Robinson was not taken up by the reigning literary clique. They may also help to explain a self-conscious literariness that hangs about some of his work. A poem such as "Many Are Called" has something of the autodidact about it, and others seem to exist more as proof that the academic deficiencies have been made good than because Robinson has anything important to say.

Yet although Robinson achieved no literary fame at Harvard—and indeed after two years he was forced to leave and return to his impoverished family in Gardiner, Maine—the atmosphere he encountered during his university years obviously encouraged him in his determination to succeed as an American poet. That determination was strong enough to carry him through years of poverty, hardship and neglect. It created in him an unswerving loyalty to his craft and a fierce pride in his vocation. One result of this was that when Theodore Roosevelt interceded to get him finally settled in a decent job, Robinson chose to regard Roosevelt's action as that of a patron which required him to honour his part by writing poems on national affairs (they are nearly all poor), and by showing himself capable of steady work at his art. He therefore made it a duty to publish volumes at regular intervals for the rest of his life. But Robinson's early experiences left their scar on him. He held himself aloof from public displays of friendship or admiration. I have been told that when, in 1934, he was to go to New York from his home in Boston to receive a literary award, he deliberately evaded the party of well-wishers that Merrill Moore had organised at Boston station to cheer him on his way. Very probably it is his own sufferings that are reflected in his lifelong interest in those defeated yet unyielding figures who people so many of his poems.

In 1896 Robinson published at his own expense a volume of poems called *The Torrent and the Night Before*. The following year he paid a vanity publisher to bring out *The Children of the Night*, which duplicated work from the earlier volume and added seventeen new poems. Neither volume brought him the slightest attention, and indeed this only began with *Captain Craig and Other Poems* in 1902. For though Moody and Stickney might be encouraging new poetry at Harvard, the public at large was still looking for poetry which would prove its worth by looking nearly as good as English verse. And so, in the same year that Robinson published *The Children of the Night*, John Bannister Tabb brought out to considerable applause his third volume of poems called, simply enough, *Lyrics*. Here is an entirely representative poem from that collected, "My Secret":

> 'Tis not what I am fain to hide,
>   That doth in deepest darkness dwell,
> But what my tongue hath often tried,
>   Alas, in vain, to tell.

Tabb throughout his life was a well-received poet, and he continued to enjoy a reputation at least until the publication in 1926 of Robert Shafer's two-volume anthology of *American Literature*. Shafer called Tabb a true poet who "deserves to be read and remembered" (Pattee, by the way, had said that Tabb's lyrics possessed "beauty and finish and often distinction"). *Lyrics* had a generous press. But this poem met with silence:

> Whenever Richard Cory went down town,
> We people on the pavement looked at him;
> He was a gentleman from sole to crown,
> Clean favored, and imperially slim.
>
> And he was always quietly arrayed,
> And he was always human when he talked;
> But still he fluttered pulses when he said,
> "Good morning," and he glittered when he walked.
>
> And he was rich—yes, richer than a king—
> And admirably schooled in every grace:
> In fine, we thought that he was everything
> To make us wish that we were in his place.
>
> So on we worked, and waited for the light,
> And went without the meat, and cursed the bread;
> And Richard Cory, one calm summer night,
> Went home and put a bullet through his head.

Well, it isn't a perfect poem, but it is certainly a remarkable one and especially if you think of it beside "My Secret." It has the plain-jane manner that Robinson loves to affect and as a result of which he gains for himself just the right amount of freedom to let otherwise unremarkable phrases stand out. Taken in context, the phrase "imperially slim," for example, has an almost sensuous, supple, and therefore slightly mocking grace about it. "Richard Cory" is wry, grim, laconic: it is a typical Robinsonian perception of the bleak comedy of the human condition, and this perception features in much of his best—and worst—work. In addition, the poem has that first-rate anecdotal quality which Robinson shares with Hardy.

Hardy, in fact, was a congenial poet, and Robinson shares some of the Englishman's least impressive and most imitable tactics and attitudes; he too has his poems about life's little ironies, and remarkably predictable they are. More importantly, however, he also shares with Hardy the ability to tell a story in verse in such a way as to let the smallest and most insignificant detail take on meaning and value. (Even the "calm" summer night in "Richard Cory" isn't quite the irrelevant detail it may at first seem, though the point it is making is admittedly an obvious one.) But another English poet was still more congenial. In his first volume, Robinson published a sonnet on George Crabbe, and it shows just how exactly he had taken Crabbe's measure. Crabbe has been forgotten by later poets, Robinson says, and yet his real value is desperately needed and cannot be dismissed (a claim Pound was to make some twenty years later). Crabbe's

> hard, human pulse is throbbing still
> With the sure strength that fearless truth endows

and we should never forget or deny Crabbe's enviable possession of "plain excellence and stubborn skill." The praise not only memorably catches Crabbe's especial distinction, it points to Robinson's very similar strengths. For Crabbe's "plain excellence" is of course that of the unadorned style. Moreover, the phrase has a sly wit to it, it hints at the unarguable fact of that excellence, and this laconic turn of expression is also common to both men.

In the last analysis, Crabbe's human pulse is the harder. Robinson, like Moody and Stickney, was more apt to be under the sway of the eternal sadness of things. (Though unlike them he wasn't trying to demonstrate this as a cultivated stance, so that his sadness—whether wry, grim or resigned— is more authentic than theirs.) But for all their differences, Robinson shares with Crabbe the ability to write memorably and truthfully about certain very ordinary people. Robinson's people belong to Tilbury, that small New England town clearly modeled on Gardiner; he brings his open-eyed awe to bear on them so intently that he becomes their special poet. He is the first and still the best poet-historian of this essential part of America, just as Sarah Orne Jewett is its first prose historian. (Her collection of stories, *The Country of the Pointed Firs*, about the Maine fishing village Dunnet Landing, appeared in 1898). Because he is the first to write about them, the people he puts into his work are for the first time given an identity in literature. Adam naming the animals, perhaps. Yet the formulation won't really do, because Robinson's eye isn't as innocent as all that; for though his reverence for the quotidian of life suggests something of the sheer wonder of being human at this time and in this place, he tends to focus on moments of sadness, of deprivation and loss. This can be seen here, in "Reuben Bright," an entirely typical and honourable performance:

> Because he was a butcher and thereby
> Did earn an honest living (and did right),
> I would not have you think that Reuben Bright
> Was any more a brute than you or I;
> For when they told him that his wife must die,
> He stared at them, and shook with grief and fright,
> And made the women cry to see him cry.
>
> And after she was dead, and he had paid
> The Singers and the sexton and the rest,
> He packed a lot of things that she had made
> Most mournfully away in an old chest
> Of hers, and put some chopped-up cedar boughs
> In with them, and tore down the slaughter-house.

And . . . and . . . and. A story, Forster said, tells you what happened next; it amounts to saying "and then." A plot tells you *why* something happened next. "Reuben Bright" is a story which has the hint of a plot running through it. The poet doesn't try to interpret the events, he merely sets down how one thing followed on from another, and his tone is seemingly neutral and detached. But inside the tiny anecdote we are allowed to guess at the connection of events and to feel how Reuben Bright's behaviour has been affected almost to madness by his wife's death. He may well appear a "brute" (even his name feels as though it should contract to the word), yet Robinson tells us a great deal about the butcher's crude tenderness of regard in the detail of the "chopped-up cedar boughs." To get away with that a poet must be able to speak without a hint of condescension, and he must also care so passionately for our having the exact facts of the case that he will be prepared to risk the near-bathetic enjambment on "an old chest / Of hers." Who cares whose chest it is? Robinson, of course, just as he cares that his audience shouldn't snigger at Reuben Bright. Why else that inscrutable tone of the opening lines, which is hardly chosen to put an audience at its ease? What it does is to guard against any possibility that Reuben Bright, the small-town epitome of the Protestant ethic, could be dismissed as humanly uninteresting or trivially corrupt. The tone feels at first merely prim, but the more you study it, the slyer it becomes and the more difficult to pin down. It guarantees precisely the grudged interest in its subject that a more defenceless tone might lose. Not that I am wanting to put Robinson forward as defendant of the Protestant ethic; he is more properly described as its sardonic satirist (as in "Cassandra"), and after all, it was he who wrote that wicked sonnet on "New England":

> Passion is here a soilure of the wits,
> We're told, and Love a cross for them to bear;
> Joy shivers in the corner where she knits
> And Conscience always has the easy chair,
> Cheerful as when she tortured into fits
> The first cat that was ever killed by Care.

But Robinson is also determined that there shall be no snobbish dismissal of the people he wants to record in his poetry. "Miniver Cheevy" is a fair example of his ability to identify and discomfort the enemy.

It is when you are alerted to Robinson's generous fair-mindedness, the intelligent humility that characterises his attitude to the people he writes about, that you become conscious of just where he is a better poet than Frost. Even Randall Jarrell, Frost's most eloquent admirer, was forced to acknowledge the lack of generosity, the hard vanity and complacency that mar so much of Frost's writing. Robinson has none of these faults. Indeed if it were not for his wit, he would be a peculiarly self-effacing poet. The reason is not hard to find. It lies in the fact that he is so absorbed in the lives he records that his art goes into rendering his characters with all the love, skill and justice he can muster. What Rilke said about works of art applies exactly to Robinson's way with the inhabitants of Tilbury Town. "Works of art," Rilke wrote to his young friend Kappus, "are of an infinite loneliness and with nothing so little to be reached as with criticism. Only love can grasp and hold and be just towards them." Substitute "people" for "works of art" and you have Robinson's attitude to perfection. Poem after poem testifies to his loving concern to be just to his characters, and through all of them runs the hesitant conviction that people are of an infinite loneliness, since they can never communicate the ultimate truth that the poet is called upon to utter—that life is marked by the defeat of hopes through the agencies of death, of time, or of what he vaguely calls "Destiny." When Robinson is riding the idea of destiny too hard, his poems tend to sink towards a lugubrious sadness; but others, like "Calverly's" and "Clavering," have the note of resigned, impersonal wisdom that we find in Hardy's "An Ancient to Ancients" and "During Wind and Rain." And such a poem as "For a Dead Lady" survives its worst prosiness to become an unforgettable statement about the ravages of time in the great, apparently plain but in fact singing, humming manner of Turberville or Gascoigne. Here is the last stanza:

> The beauty, shattered by the laws
> That have creation in their keeping,
> No longer trembles at applause,
> Or over children that are sleeping;
> And we who delve in beauty's lore
> Know all that we have known before
> Of what inexorable cause
> Makes Time so vicious in his reaping.

Many of Robinson's poems succeed in this way. Turn to any of his volumes and you will find that it is so. Above all, there is "Mr Flood's Party." But what can a critic hope to say about this poem? That it is one of the most beautifully considerate, tender poems about loneliness ever written; that it combines wit and pathos in a way that makes it intensely sympathetic and yet scrupulously intelligent towards its subject? As for its tone—Conrad Aiken once remarked that Robinson's characteristic tone hovered somewhere between the ironic and the elegiac, and this is perhaps as near as we can come to catching the tone of "Mr Flood's Party." The poem is about a lonely, ageing drunkard, a disreputable outcast from his community, more comic than pitiful, a man who has kept his dissolute wits about him. But though Robinson doesn't waste any pity on Mr Flood, sympathy is powerfully present by virtue of the attentiveness, the plain excellence that sets down his story:

> Old Eben Flood, climbing alone one night
> Over the hill between the town below
> And the forsaken upland hermitage
> That held as much as he should ever know
> On earth again of home, paused warily.

It is the withheld word that does the trick: not wearily, but "warily." This old man has too much native wit to be the object of sentimental pity. For Robinson to draw our attention to this fact is proof enough of the comic regard in which he holds Mr Flood, but it surely emerges in the very way the story opens. How can you resist a poem that starts as this one does? It is so compelling, so much in the manner of the born storyteller. As the poem continues, the tale becomes more comic, more outrageously strange, more humanly fascinating. Robinson is so completely in command that he can switch the changes in the third stanza from the near-mocking grandilo-quence of the opening lines to the closing lines, which shame our smiles:

> Alone, as if enduring to the end
> A valiant armor of scarred hopes outworn,
> He stood there in the middle of the road
> Like Roland's ghost winding a silent horn.
> Below him, in the town among the trees,
> Where friends of other days had honoured him,
> A phantom salutation of the dead
> Rang thinly till old Eben's eyes were dim.

Yet the closing lines clearly need the bracing effect of the mock-heroic that plays about the first half-stanza if they are not to stray into mere pathos. And consider how much Robinson risks, and brings off, in the fourth stanza:

> Then, as a mother lays her sleeping child
> Down tenderly, fearing it may awake,
> He set the jug down slowly at his feet
> With trembling care, knowing that most things break;
> And only when assured that on firm earth
> It stood, as the uncertain lives of men
> Assuredly did not, he paced away,
> And with his hand extended paused again:

The control of language in that stanza is as perfect as anyone could wish for. The simile of the tipsy old man setting his jug down, like a mother, with "trembling care," is so audacious and yet so obviously written out of regard for him and not for cleverness' sake, that it doesn't seem the least bit inge-nious or self-regarding. Moreover, the laconic phrase, "knowing that most things break," strikes me as exactly the sort of triumph that Robinson's style can bring him: it quite miraculously holds the balance between the poet's resistance to bathos and his need to honour that slightly indulgent but sure

knowledge that Mr Flood carries with him. So it is with the rest of the
poem. But here I have simply to quote:

> "Well, Mr Flood, we have not met like this
> In a long time; and many a change has come
> To both of us, I fear, since last it was
> We had a drop together. Welcome home!"
> Convivially returning with himself,
> Again he raised the jug up to the light;
> And with an acquiescent quaver said:
> "Well, Mr Flood, if you insist, I might."
>
> "Only a very little, Mr Flood—
> For auld lang syne. No more, sir; that will do."
> So, for the time, apparently it did,
> And Eben evidently thought so too;
> For soon amid the silver loneliness
> Of night he lifted up his voice and sang,
> Secure, with only two moons listening,
> Until the whole harmonious landscape rang—
>
> "For auld lang syne." The weary throat gave out,
> The last words wavered; and the song being done,
> He raised again the jug regretfully
> And shook his head, and was again alone.
> There was not much that was ahead of him,
> And there was nothing in the town below—
> Where strangers would have shut the many doors
> That many friends had opened long ago.

There is really nothing to say about that, except how wonderful it is. You
can note the great line "There was not much that was ahead of him," the
wit that is unwaveringly attentive towards Eben's caution ("Secure, with
only two moons listening"), the comic "Convivially returning with himself"; and so on. But ticking off the points that make "Mr Flood's Party" a
masterpiece comes to feel a very trivial exercise. What perhaps is worth
saying is that it is precisely because Robinson finds such scenes worth recording that he is so invaluable a poet. For the subject of "Mr Flood's
Party" hardly seems to warrant a poem at all and certainly not the major
poem that Robinson fashions. Yet it is just because of his shrewd, sad, but

comically receptive open-eyed awe that Robinson *can* find the right way of recording his ordinary citizens. This is his distinctive role as poet: he is spokesman for the inarticulate, for those who, whatever the reason, have been forced into incommunicable loneliness. So he becomes the historian of people as Masters, with his slick cynicism, and Sandburg, all squashily sentimental, could not hope to be. "Mr Flood's Party" belongs not with them but with the Frost of "Home Burial" and "Death of the Hired Man," which is not to deny that Frost is the greater poet. It is, however, to say that Robinson deserves to be set beside the great poets of the language.

Figures like Mr Flood recur throughout Robinson's poetry, even when he is not writing about Tilbury Town. Not all of them are comic, but they have in common the fact that invariably they are old men who have known repeated disappointments and defeats and yet have sufficient resilience to journey on to the defeat of whatever hopes are left to them. They include the Dutchman, the Wandering Jew and Rembrandt. All of them possess the Jew's "old, unyielding eyes," and they are therefore far too tough to surrender to their gnawing self-doubts. It is, of course, utterly characteristic of Robinson that he should have written a monologue for the Rembrandt of the late self-portraits. Clearly he recognised those great remorseless studies for what they are: indomitable self-scrutinies that triumph by their willingness to face and acknowledge the worst. Robinson's Rembrandt is perhaps rather less fiercely courageous than his real-life counterpart; and for that reason the poem does not provide the great kick at misery that Rembrandt's self-portraits do. But it does testify to Robinson's ceaseless curiosity about human nature, his wanting to track down the way a man thinks and suffers and lives in his mind.

There are occasions when this brings him face to face with a blank wall. The monologue given to Ben Jonson, in which Jonson is made to tell of his acquaintance with Shakespeare, ends in disappointment because there is nothing Robinson can have Jonson say that we don't already know; and Robinson is clearly not the poet to invent when he is dealing with the actual. With Rembrandt he has the paintings to help him; but with Shakespeare there is really nothing, once he has decided not to see Prospero as an autobiographical figure, or *Measure for Measure* as written in time of personal distress. Accordingly, Robinson's best monologue and narrative poems are the ones which are entirely works of invention. Though many are too slight and respectful to the mundane, a few stand out as among the supreme achievements of their kind. Of all the narrative poems, "Isaac and Archibald" is the surest triumph.

It has its faults, of course, and they are very representative ones. There are, for example, moments when diction and cadence imitate Tennyson imitating Wordsworth:

> and the world
> Was wide, and there was gladness everywhere.

Some lines are blatantly stuffed out to fill up the pentameter:

> At the end of an hour's walking after that
> The cottage of old Archibald appeared.
> Little and white and high on a smooth round hill
> It stood.

Once or twice the poem falls into unfocused Miltonics, as when the narrator tells of going down to Archibald's cellar:

> down we went
> Out of the fiery sunshine to the gloom,
> Grateful and half sepulchral

Yet the flaws stand for amazingly little compared with what the poem achieves. In outline, at least, it is simplicity itself. A man recalls a summer day of his childhood when he had gone with an old man, Isaac, to see the man's equally aged friend, Archibald. As they walk along, Isaac tells the boy he is worried Archibald will not have cut his field of oats, and this is the pretext for him to add that he is certain Archibald will shortly die. "The twilight warning of experience" has made him aware, he says, that "Archibald is going." But when they arrive at Archibald's cottage they find the field of oats newly cut and a spruce Archibald extending them a ready welcome. Isaac goes for a walk and instructs Archibald to stay "and rest your back and tell the boy / A story." Archibald does so, and he also tells the boy that he fears Isaac will shortly die. "I have seen it come / These eight years," he says. Isaac returns, and the two old men play cards while the boy daydreams and keeps score for them. And that is all.

But no account of this tale can hope to do justice to its beauty and integrity of manner. It tells of loneliness and the defeat of hopes; but it is also full of humorous warmth. And it is considerably less simple than appears. For it isn't only that Isaac and Archibald upset each other's point of view and in so doing comically illustrate the difficulties of truthful communication (are they lying or mistaken?); behind their words is the fear of death that neither can quite bring himself to voice. Yet the old men are not defenceless objects of pity. Like Mr Flood, they still have their wits about

them. As the boy observes, when he is striding along in the fatiguing heat
with Isaac:

> First I was half inclined
> To caution him that he was growing old
> But something that was not compassion soon
> Made plain the folly of all subterfuge.

The old men are also partly comic creations. This is not just a matter
of their anxious solicitude for what each insists is the other's failing health.
It is more, because the poem is everywhere soaked in the affectionate
comedy of observation. As here, early on:

> The sun
> Was hot, and I was ready to sweat blood;
> But Isaac, for aught I could make of him,
> Was cool to his hat-band. So I said then
> Something about the scorching days we have
> In August without knowing it sometimes;
> But Isaac said the day was like a dream,
> And praised the Lord, and talked about the breeze.

Isaac praises the Lord a good deal, and especially when he is drinking Archibald's cider:

> "I never twist a spigot nowadays,"
> He said, and raised the glass up to the light,
> "But I thank God for orchards."

Archibald is also fond of his own cider, which he declares to be newly
tapped and "an honor to the fruit." Under a barrel

> Glimmered a late-spilled proof that Archibald
> Had spoken from unfeigned experience.

But neither Isaac nor Archibald is a figure of fun. The comedy of this
poem is in no sense reductive. On the contrary, its observations and memories let us in on the affectionate regard with which the narrator holds the
old men. Take this, for example:

> There was a fluted antique water-glass
> Close by, and in it, prisoned, or at rest,
> There was a cricket, of the brown soft sort,
> That feeds on darkness. Isaac turned him out,

And touched him with his thumb to make him jump,
And then composedly pulled out the plug
With such a practised hand that scarce a drop
Did even touch his fingers.

That tells us a great deal about Isaac, just as we are told much of value
about Archibald when his

                                                     dry voice
          Cried thinly, with unpatronizing triumph
          "I've got you, Isaac, high, low, jack, and the game!"

The poem is full of these loving observations, and if that were all there
was to it "Isaac and Archibald" would still be a considerable achievement.
But there is so much else. In the first place, we are bound to notice the
elegiac air that hangs over it, and which supplies us with the clear hint that
the narrator is drawn to his memories because he has found his life very
different from the innocent and hopeful daydreams in which he indulged
while Isaac and Archibald were playing cards:

                              Now and then my fancy caught
          A flying glimpse of a good life beyond—
          Something of ships and sunlight, streets and singing,
          Troy falling and the ages coming back,
          And ages coming forward: Archibald
          And Isaac were good fellows in old clothes,
          And Agamemnon was a friend of mine:
          Ulysses coming home again to shoot
          With bows and feathered arrows made another,
          And all was as it should be. I was young.

Going with this hint of defeated hopes is the suggestion that he has come
to a saddening recognition of the limits of friendship. In his childhood
dreams he was the friend of Agamemnon and Ulysses, but now, years later,
he is led to recall the two old friends who had been unable to communicate
their fears of death to each other. He also, of course, realises that life isn't
art or literature.

But what more than anything stands out from the memories of that
far-off day is the fact of loneliness. Isaac tells the boy that he cannot expect
to understand "the singular idea of loneliness." It is a paradoxical effort at
communication, and both Isaac and Archibald talk to the boy in the hope
of making him understand their own predicaments. Thus Archibald tells

him to remember what he has said about "the light behind the stars." Yet
he knows the boy cannot understand his words and what they imply:

> "But there, there,
> I'm going it again, as Isaac says,
> And I'll stop now before you go to sleep—
> Only be sure that you growl cautiously,
> And always where the shadow may not reach you."
> Never shall I forget, long as I live,
> The quaint thin crack in Archibald's voice,
> The lonely twinkle in his little eyes,
> Or the way it made me feel to be with him.

Beyond all else, the old men want to be remembered. Archibald says to the
boy, "Remember that: remember that I said it." But the actual words are
not really what he's talking about; for, facing the ultimate loneliness of
death, the old man wants somehow to be assured that his identity will survive in another person's acceptance of him. And the same holds true for
Isaac. He says:

> "Look at me, my boy,
> And when the time shall come for you to see
> That I must follow after him, try then
> To think of me, to bring me back again,
> Just as I was today. Think of the place
> Where we are sitting now, and think of me—
> Think of old Isaac as you knew him then,
> When you set out with him in August once
> To see old Archibald."—The words come back
> Almost as Isaac must have uttered them.

"*Almost* as Isaac *must* have uttered them." The narrator of this poem is too
truthful not to accept that much that Isaac and Archibald hoped would be
saved in fact had to die with them.

But it would be wrong to give the impression that the poem settles
merely for the sadness of incommunicable isolation. While acknowledging
that this must be so, it also pays tribute to the power of human regard that
in some measure, at least, triumphs over the loneliness in which each person
must be trapped. For the narrator honours and celebrates Isaac and Archibald simply by the vitality of memories that clamber from years of neglect
in order to testify to the enduring warmth of affection he has for the old
men, and the memories savour the cadences of remembered speech so that

the old men return almost like Hardy's ghosts. Besides, the poem doesn't end on a dying fall but with a last hint of a companionship that almost throughout had seemed beyond reach:

> I knew them and I may have laughed at them;
> But there's a laughing that has honor in it,
> And I have no regrets for light words now.
> Rather I think sometimes they may have made
> Their sport of me;—but they would not do that,
> They were too old for that. They were old men,
> And I may laugh at them because I knew them.

These last lines are beautifully just; they bring the poem to a close by accepting the inscrutability of human behaviour at the same time as matching it with the kind of knowledge derived from a source that implies communication. They suggest a good deal about Robinson's characteristic method. For if, like his admired Crabbe, Robinson is the poet of plain realities, he is also like Crabbe the poet of surprises, and these are likely to show themselves in the precise ways he responds to the mysteriousness of people, no matter how ordinary they may seem. This is the hallmark of an unfailing curiosity, and it makes Robinson one of the necessary poets.

Chronology

1869   Edwin Arlington Robinson born on December 22 at Head Tide, Maine, the third son (after Dean and Herman) of Edward and Mary Palmer.

1870   Robinson's family moves to Gardiner, Maine, in September.

1884–88   At Gardiner High School, Robinson becomes acquainted with Alanson Tucker Schumann, a teacher who introduces him to the "Club," a small, local literary group.

1889   Robinson spends a postgraduate year at Gardiner High School studying Horace and Milton.

1891–93   Robinson attends Harvard as a special student and publishes poems in the *Harvard Advocate*.

1892   Robinson's father dies.

1893–96   Robinson's family suffers financial difficulties. Robinson stays in Gardiner, writing poetry, and tries to write and sell short stories with little success. He translates *Antigone* with Harry de Forest Smith.

1896   At his own expense, Robinson prints *The Torrent and the Night Before*. His mother dies of "black diphtheria."

1897   Robinson lives in New York for a short time and publishes *The Children of the Night*.

1899   Robinson works as a secretary in the office of President Eliot of Harvard from January to June and then returns to New York. In September his brother Dean dies, presumably a suicide.

1902	*Captain Craig* published, after being rejected by five publishers.
1903–4	Robinson works as a time-checker during the construction of New York's first subway.
1905–9	Theodore Roosevelt comes across *The Children of the Night* through his son and writes a critical estimate of the poetry in *The Outlook*. *The Children of the Night* is reprinted. The President appoints Robinson to a position in the New York office of the Collector of Customs. Robinson attempts to write plays, *Van Zorn* and *Porcupine,* for the New York stage. His brother Herman dies.
1910	*The Town down the River* published.
1911	Robinson spends the first of twenty-four summers at the MacDowell Colony in Peterborough, New Hampshire.
1914	*Van Zorn* published.
1915	*Captain Craig* reprinted.
1916	Robinson publishes *The Man against the Sky.*
1917	*Merlin,* Robinson's first book-length Arthurian poem, published.
1919	The *New York Times Book Review* honors Robinson on his fiftieth birthday with tributes from his contemporaries.
1920	*Lancelot* and *The Three Taverns* published.
1921	*Avon's Harvest* published. Robinson's *Collected Poems* wins the Pulitzer Prize.
1923	*Roman Bartholow* published. Robinson visits England.
1924	*The Man Who Died Twice* is published and awarded a Pulitzer Prize.
1925	Robinson publishes *Dionysus in Doubt.*
1927	*Tristram,* Robinson's third Arthurian epic, becomes a bestseller. Robinson awarded his third Pulitzer Prize.
1929–34	Robinson publishes *Cavender's House, The Glory of the*

Nightingales, Selected Poems, Matthias at the Door, Nicodemus, Talifer, Amaranth.

1935 Robinson dies on April 6, in New York Hospital. *King Jasper* published posthumously with an introduction by Robert Frost.

Contributors

HAROLD BLOOM, Sterling Professor of the Humanities at Yale University, is the author of *The Anxiety of Influence, Poetry and Repression,* and many other volumes of literary criticism. His forthcoming study, *Freud: Transference and Authority,* attempts a full-scale reading of all of Freud's major writings. A MacArthur Prize Fellow, he is general editor of five series of literary criticism published by Chelsea House. During 1987–88, he served as Charles Eliot Norton Professor of Poetry at Harvard University.

YVOR WINTERS wrote numerous critical studies, including *In Defense of Reason.* He also published eleven volumes of verse. Winters spent most of his teaching career at Stanford University. He died in 1968.

ROY HARVEY PEARCE is Professor of American Literature at the University of California at San Diego. A fellow of the American Academy of Arts and Sciences, his books include *The Savages of America* and *Historicism Once More: Problems and Occasions for the American Scholar.*

DENIS DONOGHUE is Henry James Professor of English and American Literature at New York University. His books include *Thieves of Fire* and *Ferocious Alphabets.*

JAMES DICKEY is Professor of English and poet-in-residence at the University of South Carolina. His fourth volume of poems, *Buckdancer's Choice,* won a National Book Award.

HYATT H. WAGGONER is the author of *American Poets from the Puritans to the Present,* among other studies of American literature.

NATHAN COMFORT STARR is Professor Emeritus of English and Humanities at the University of Florida. He is the author of *The Dynamics of Literature* and *King Arthur Today.*

IRVING HOWE is Distinguished Professor of English at Hunter College of the City University of New York. He is the editor of *Dissent* and the author of numerous books of literary criticism and political and cultural commentary.

JOSEPHINE MILES spent most of her teaching career at the University of California, Berkeley. Her *Selected Poems* won the Pulitzer Prize in 1984.

JOHN LUCAS is Professor of English and Drama at the University of Loughborough, Leicestershire. He is the author of several volumes of literary essays, including *The Literature of Change*.

Bibliography

Aiken, Conrad. *Collected Criticism*. New York: Oxford University Press, 1968.

Anderson, Wallace L. *Edwin Arlington Robinson: A Critical Introduction*. Boston: Houghton Mifflin, 1967.

Baker, Carlos. "'The Jug Makes Paradise': New Light on Eben Flood." *Colby Library Quarterly* 10 (1974):327–36.

———. "Robinson's Stoical Romanticism: 1890–1897." *New England Quarterly* 46 (1973): 3–16.

Barnard, Ellsworth. *Edwin Arlington Robinson: A Critical Study*. New York: Octagon Books, 1969.

Bates, Esther Willard. *Edwin Arlington Robinson and His Manuscripts*. Waterville, Maine: Colby College Library, 1944.

Bedell, R. Meredith. "Perception, Action, and Life in *The Man against the Sky*." *Colby Library Quarterly* 12 (1976): 29–37.

Budd, Louise J. "E. A. Robinson Unbends for Academe." *Colby Library Quarterly* 16 (1980): 248–51.

Cary, Richard, ed. *Appreciation of Edwin Arlington Robinson*. Waterville, Maine: Colby College Press, 1969.

———, ed. *Edwin Arlington Robinson's Letters to Edith Brower*. Cambridge: Harvard University Press, 1968.

———. "Robinson's Friend Arthur Davis Variell." *Colby Library Quarterly* 10 (1974): 372–85.

Cestre, Charles. *An Introduction to Edwin Arlington Robinson*. New York: Macmillan, 1930.

Clark, S. L., and Julian N. Wasserman. "'Time Is a Casket': Love and Temporality in Robinson's *Tristram*." *Colby Library Quarterly* 17 (1981): 112–16.

Colby Library Quarterly 8, nos. 1–4 (1969). Special Robinson issue.

Cox, Don R. "The Vision of Robinson's Merlin." *Colby Library Quarterly* 10 (1974): 495–504.

Coxe, Louise O. *Edwin Arlington Robinson: The Life of Poetry*. New York: Pegasus, 1969.

———. *Robinson*. Minneapolis: University of Minnesota Press, 1962.

Crowder, Richard. "The Emergence of E. A. Robinson." *The South Atlantic Quarterly* 45 (1946): 89.

Cunningham, J. V. "Edwin Arlington Robinson: A Brief Biography." In *The Collected Essays of J. V. Cunningham,* 375–78. Chicago: Swallow, 1976.

Donaldson, Scott. "The Alien Pity: A Study of the Characters in E. A. Robinson." *American Literature* 38 (1966): 219–29.

Dunn, N. E. "'Riddling Leaves': Robinson's 'Luke Havergal.'" *Colby Library Quarterly* 10 (1973): 17–25.

Edwards, C. Hines, Jr. "Allusion and Symbol in Robinson's 'Eros Turannos.'" *Colby Library Quarterly* 20 (1984): 47–50.

Fish, Robert S. "The Tempering of Faith in E. A. Robinson's 'The Man against the Sky.'" *Colby Library Quarterly* 9 (1972): 441–55.

Franchere, Hoyt. *Edwin Arlington Robinson.* New York: Twayne, 1968.

Free, William J. "E. A. Robinson's Use of Emerson." *American Literature* 38 (1966): 69–84.

Frost, Robert. Introduction to *King Jasper,* by Edwin Arlington Robinson. New York: Macmillan, 1935.

Fussell, Edwin S. *Edwin Arlington Robinson: The Literary Background of a Traditional Poet.* Berkeley and Los Angeles: University of California Press, 1954.

Hagedorn, Herman. *Edwin Arlington Robinson.* New York: Macmillan, 1938.

Joyner, Nancy Carol. "Addenda to Hogan and White: E. A. Robinson." *Papers of the Bibliographical Society of America* 72 (1978): 246–47.

Kart, Lawrence. "Richard Cory: Artist without an Art." *Colby Library Quarterly* 11 (1975): 160–61.

Kavka, Jerome. "Richard Cory's Suicide: A Psychoanalyst's View." *Colby Library Quarterly* 11 (1975): 150–59.

McCoy, Dorothy Schuman. "The Arthurian Strain in Early Twentieth Century Literature: Cabell, T. S. Eliot, and E. A. Robinson." *West Virginia University Philological Papers* 28 (1982): 95–104.

McFarland, Ronald E. "Robinson's 'Luke Havergal.'" *Colby Library Quarterly* 10 (1974): 365–72.

Manheimer, Joan. "Edwin Arlington Robinson's 'Eros Turannos': Narrative Reconsidered." *The Literary Review* 20 (1977): 253–69.

Miller, John H. "The Structure of E. A. Robinson's *The Torrent and the Night Before.*" *Colby Library Quarterly* 10 (1974): 347–64.

Montiero, George. "'The President and The Poet': Robinson, Roosevelt, and *The Touchstone.*" *Colby Library Quarterly* 10 (1974): 512–14.

Morris, Celia. "E. A. Robinson and the Golden Horoscope of Imperfection." *Colby Library Quarterly* 11 (1975): 88–97.

———. "Robinson's Camelot: Renunciation as Drama." *Colby Library Quarterly* 9(1972): 468–82.

Murphy, Francis, ed. *Edwin Arlington Robinson: A Collection of Critical Essays.* Englewood Cliffs, N.J.: Prentice-Hall, 1970.

Neff, Emery, *Edwin Arlington Robinson.* New York: William Sloane Associates, 1948.

Perrine, Laurence. "The Sources of Robinson's Arthurian Poems and His Opinions of Other Treatments." *Colby Library Quarterly* 10 (1974): 336–46.

Pritchard, William H. "Edwin Arlington Robinson: The Prince of Heartaches." In

The Lives of Modern Poets, 83–107. New York: Oxford University Press, 1980.

Redman, Ben Ray. *Edwin Arlington Robinson.* New York: R. M. McBride, 1926.

Robinson, William R. *Edwin Arlington Robinson: A Poetry of the Act.* Cleveland: University Press of Case Western Reserve, 1967.

Samply, Arthur M. "The Power or the Glory: The Dilemma of Edwin Arlington Robinson." *Colby Library Quarterly* 9 (1971): 357–66.

Sanborn, John N. "Juxtaposition as Structure in 'The Man against the Sky.'" *Colby Library Quarterly* 10 (1974): 486–94.

Shinn, Thelma J. "The Art of a Verse Novelist: Approaching Robinson's Late Narratives through James's *The Art of the Novelist.*" *Colby Library Quarterly* 12 (1976): 91–100.

Smith, Chard Powers. *Where the Light Falls: A Portrait of Edwin Arlington Robinson.* New York: Macmillan, 1965.

Spear, Jeffrey L. "Robinson, Hardy, and a Literary Source of 'Eros Turannos.'" *Colby Library Quarterly* 15 (1979): 58–64.

Starr, Nathan Comfort. "Edwin Arlington Robinson's Arthurian Heroines: Vivian, Guinevere, and the Two Isolts." *Philological Quarterly* 56 (1977): 253–58.

Sutcliffe, Denham, ed. *Untriangulated Stars: Letters of Edwin Arlington Robinson to Harry DeForest Smith, 1890–1905.* Cambridge: Harvard University Press, 1968.

Tate, Allen. *On the Limits of Poetry.* New York: Swallow, 1948.

Torrence, Ridgely, ed. *Selected Letters of Edwin Arlington Robinson.* New York: Macmillan, 1940.

Untermeyer, Louis. *Edwin Arlington Robinson: A Reappraisal.* Washington, D.C.: Library of Congress, 1963.

Van Doren, Mark. *Edwin Arlington Robinson.* New York: Literary Guild, 1927.

Waggoner, Hyatt H. "E. A. Robinson and the Cosmic Chill." *New England Quarterly* 13 (1940): 65–84.

Winters, Yvor. *Edwin Arlington Robinson.* Norfolk, Conn.: New Directions, 1946.

Wolf, H. R. "E. A. Robinson and the Integration of Self." In *Modern American Poetry: Essays on Criticism,* edited by Jerome Mazzaro, 40–59. New York: David Mckay Co., 1970.

Acknowledgments

"Introduction" (originally entitled "Bacchus and Merlin: The Dialectic of Poetry in America") by Harold Bloom from *The Ringers in the Tower* by Harold Bloom, © 1971 by the University of Chicago. Reprinted by permission of the University of Chicago Press.

"A Cool Master" by Yvor Winters from *Yvor Winters: Uncollected Essays and Reviews* by Yvor Winters, © 1973 by Janet Lewis Winters. Published by The Swallow Press. Reprinted by permission of Ohio University Press.

"The Old Poetry and the New: Robinson" (originally entitled "The Old Poetry and the New") by Roy Harvey Pearce from *The Continuity of American Poetry* by Roy Harvey Pearce, © 1961 by Princeton University Press. Reprinted by permission of Princeton University Press.

"A Poet of Continuing Relevance" (originally entitled "Edwin Arlington Robinson, J. V. Cunningham, Robert Lowell") by Denis Donoghue from *Connoisseurs of Chaos* by Denis Donoghue, © 1964, 1984 by Denis Donoghue. Reprinted by permission of the author and Columbia University Press.

"Edwin Arlington Robinson: The Many Truths" (originally entitled "Introduction") by James Dickey from *Selected Poems of Edwin Arlington Robinson*, edited by Morton Dauwen Zabel, © 1965 by the Macmillan Publishing Co. Reprinted by permission of the Macmillan Publishing Co. The excerpts of Edwin Arlington Robinson's poems are reprinted by permission of the Macmillan Publishing Co. and the Scribner Publishing Co.

"The Idealist *in Extremis*" by Hyatt H. Waggoner from *American Poets: From the Puritans to the Present* (rev. ed.) by Hyatt H. Waggoner, © 1968, 1984 by Hyatt H. Waggoner. Reprinted by permission of the author and Louisiana State University Press.

"The Transformation of Merlin" by Nathan Comfort Starr from *Edwin Arlington Robinson: Centenary Essays*, edited by Ellsworth Barnard, © 1969 by the University of Georgia Press. Reprinted by permission of the University of Georgia Press.

"A Grave and Solitary Voice" by Irving Howe from *The Critical Point: On Literature and Culture* by Irving Howe, © 1973 by Irving Howe. Reprinted by permission.

"Robinson and the Years Ahead" by Josephine Miles from *Poetry and Change* by Josephine Miles, © 1974 by the Regents of the University of California. Reprinted by permission of the University of California Press.

"The Poetry of Edwin Arlington Robinson" by John Lucas from *Moderns and Contemporaries* by John Lucas, © 1985 by John Lucas. Reprinted by permission of the Harvester Press Ltd. and Barnes & Noble Books, Totowa, New Jersey.

Index

"Aaron Stark," 32, 36, 120
"Adam and Eve" (Lowell), 47–48
Adler, Alfred, 70
Aiken, Conrad, 11, 115–16, 145
Aldrich, Thomas Bailey, 15
"Altar, The," 32
Amaranth, 97; style of, 79, 98, 99;
    weaknesses of, 31, 32, 98
American 1890s (Ziff), 140
American Literature (Shafer), 141
"Ancient to Ancients, An" (Hardy),
    145
"Another Dark Lady," 32
Arnold, Matthew, 88
"At Castle Boterel" (Hardy), 123
"August Hail" (Cunningham), 42–43
"Aunt Imogen," 123
Avon's Harvest, 63, 132, 133, 134

"Bacchus," 1
Ballads (Percy), 129
Bates, Esther Willard, 134
"Battle of Hastings, The," (Chatterton),
    128–29
"Beacon, The" (Cunningham), 40–41
Beckett, Samuel, 34–35
"Ben Jonson Entertains a Man from
    Stratford," 7, 9
Bierce, Ambrose, 15
Browning, Robert, 2, 9, 62, 132
Bunner, Henry Cuyler, 15
Bunyan, John, 23
Burroughs, John, 74

Calderón de la Barca, Pedro, 77
"Calverly's," 56–58, 69, 145

"Captain Carpenter" (Ransom), 31
Captain Craig, 84, 94
"Captain Craig," 3, 94;
    characterization in, 26–27, 86–89;
    weaknesses of, 26, 30, 31
Carlyle, Thomas, 75, 76
"Cassandra," 26, 144
Cavender's House, 31, 99–100
Cawein, Madison, 15
Chatterton, Thomas, 128–30
Children of the Night, The: publication
    of, 140, 141; style of, 10, 77, 82,
    127
"Children of the Night, The," 1, 2–3,
    79
Chivers, Thomas, 134
"Christmas Banquet, The" (Haw-
    thorne), 99
"Christmas Eve under Hooker's Statue"
    (Lowell), 46, 47
"Clavering," 145
"Clerks, The," 1, 89, 120–21
"Cliff Klingenhagen," 32, 131
Cocktail Party, The (Eliot), 95, 96
Coleridge, Samuel Taylor, 41, 127–28,
    132, 134
Collected Poems, 31, 79, 83, 84. *See
    also specific poems*
"Colloquy in Black Rock" (Lowell),
    46, 48
"Concord" (Lowell), 47
Conduct of Life, The (Emerson), 1, 76,
    83, 85
Confidential Clerk, The (Eliot), 96
*Connecticut Yankee At King Arthur's
    Court, A* (Twain), 102
Country of the Pointed Firs, The (Jew-
    ett), 143

Crabbe, George, 126, 142, 153
Crane, Stephen, 15, 139
"Credo": language in, 79–80, 131; style of, 1, 3, 118
Creech, Thomas, 129
Croce, Benedetto, 6
Crowder, Richard, 15
Cunningham, J. V., 40–45

"Dark Hills, The," 90–91
"Dead Village, The," 131
"Dear Friends," 130
"Death of the Hired Man" (Frost), 148
"Demos," 37
Denham, Sir John, 129
Dickey, James, 122
Dickinson, Emily: and Emerson, 6, 98; "Last Night, The," 6; as poet, 5–6, 15, 127, 138; Robinson compared to, 73–74, 100
Dionysus in Doubt. See specific poems
"Directive," 3
"Divinity School Address" (Emerson), 27
Doolittle, Hilda, 11
Dreiser, Theodore, 74
Dunbar, Paul Laurence, 15
"During Wind and Rain" (Hardy), 145

Eddington, Sir Arthur Stanley, 78
Eddy, Mary Baker, 74
Edwin Arlington Robinson (Hagedorn), 117
Edwin Arlington Robinson and His Manuscripts (Bates), 134
Eliot, T. S.: as poet, 67, 121, 123; and Robinson, 11, 95, 96, 116. See also specific works
Emerson, Ralph Waldo: and Dickinson, 6, 98; and Frost, 1, 2, 78, 100; religion as viewed by, 73, 74, 99; and Robinson, 1, 2, 3, 20, 26, 27, 75, 76–78, 79–82, 83, 84–85, 86, 88, 89, 91, 93, 95, 96, 97, 98–99, 100, 118; transcendentalism as viewed by, 82–83, 99; as writer, 14, 20, 74, 88. See also specific works
"Envoi, L'," 131–32

"Erasmus," 84, 85–86
"Eros Turannos": characterization in, 20–22, 23; failure as theme in, 22, 116; general themes in, 2, 22–23, 91, 122–23; isolation and loneliness as themes in, 22, 116; as major work, 1, 9, 32, 53, 94; style of, 9, 22, 23, 24, 122–23
Estoire de Merlin, L' (Anonymous), 101–2
"Experience" (Emerson), 1
Experimental Novel, The (Zola), 79

Fairfax, Edward, 129
Family Reunion, The (Eliot), 35
"Fate" (Emerson), 1
Faulkner, William, 119
"Ferris Wheel, The" (Lowell), 47
Field, Eugene, 15, 139
"Flammonde," 18–19, 23
"Fleming Helphenstine," 32
"For a Dead Lady," 1, 29–30, 145
Forster, E. M., 143
"For the Union Dead" (Lowell), 139
Four Quartets (Eliot), 96
Fox, George, 83
"Fragment," 18–19
"Friendship" (Emerson), 75
Frost, Robert: and Emerson, 1, 2, 78, 100; as poet, 11, 31, 127, 144; and Robinson, 1, 3, 7, 9, 89, 90, 91, 94, 100, 122, 123, 125, 133, 135, 137, 144, 148. See also specific poems

Garland, Hamlin, 74
Gascoigne, George, 145
"George Crabbe," 142; Crabbe as viewed in, 77, 126; as major work, 1, 32.
"Gift of God, The," 23
Gilder, Richard Watson, 15, 138
"Glory of the Nightingales, The," 31–32
"Going, The" (Hardy), 123
Gould, Edward, 9–10
"Grandparents" (Lowell), 47
"Great Carbuncle, The" (Hawthorne), 99

"Growth of 'Lorraine,' The," 32
Guiney, Louise Imogen, 15, 127

Hagedorn, Herman, 134
Hardy, Thomas: as poet, 123, 127;
    Robinson compared to, 2, 37, 52–
    53, 57, 62, 123, 142, 145, 153.
    See also specific works
"Haunted House," 32
Hawthorne, Nathaniel: and Robinson,
    97, 98, 99–100, 117–18, 122. *See
    also specific works*
Heartbreak House (Shaw), 32–33
Hecht, Anthony, 134
Henderson, Lawrence J., 77–78, 85, 88
"Hillcrest," 32, 94, 123
Historia Britonum (Nennius), 101
Historia Regum Britanniae (Geoffrey of
    Monmouth), 101
*History of American Literature since
    1870, A* (Pattee), 138
"Holy Innocents, The" (Lowell), 47
"Home Burial" (Frost), 148
Hopkins, Gerald Manley, 31, 48, 68
"Horatian Ode, An" (Marvell), 43
"House on the Hill, The," 61
Housman, A. E., 127
Hovey, Richard, 15, 138

Iceman Cometh, The (O'Neill), 70
Idylls of the King, The (Tennyson),
    102, 125
"Isaac and Archibald": aging as theme
    in, 65, 123; Archibald's role in, 52,
    151–53; death as theme in, 65,
    66–67, 124, 149, 152; humor in,
    149, 150; Isaac's role in, 150–51,
    152–53; isolation and loneliness as
    themes in, 149, 151–52; as major
    work, 32, 94, 124, 148; narrator's
    role in, 150–51, 152–53; style of,
    7, 124, 148–49, 151

James, Henry, 2, 116, 122
James, William, 59, 75, 77
Jarrell, Randall, 144
Jeans, Sir James Hopwood, 78
Jeffers, Robinson, 137

Jewett, Sarah Orne, 143
"John Brown," 124

"Karma," 32
"Katherine's Dream" (Lowell), 46
Keats, John, 62
Kilmer, Joyce, 78
King, Ben, 139
King Jasper, 89; general themes in, 52,
    97; mood of, 79, 98, 118–19;
    weaknesses of, 27, 31, 98; Zoe's
    role in, 52, 97
Krapp's Last Tape (Beckett), 35

Lancelot: characterization in, 52, 125;
    general themes in, 52, 94; as major
    work, 7–8, 62, 125; structure of,
    94, 95; style of, 32, 97; weak-
    nesses of, 7, 27, 32, 92, 94, 125
Lanier, Sidney, 127
Layamon, 101
Lazarus, Emma, 138–39
"Lazarus," 94
Leaves of Grass (Whitman), 139
Lewis, C. S., 103–4
Life Studies (Lowell), 47
Longfellow, Henry Wadsworth, 2
Lord Weary's Castle (Lowell), 46, 48
"Love" (Emerson), 75
Lowell, Robert, 45–52, 122. *See also
    specific volumes and poems*
"Luke Havergal," 1–2, 10, 32, 122
Lyrics (Tabb), 141

Madness of Merlin, The (Binyon), 103
Malory, Sir Thomas, 102
Man against the Sky, The, 94
"Man against the Sky, The," 32; char-
    acterization in, 24–25, 105; gen-
    eral themes in, 26, 78; style of,
    24–25, 26, 68–69, 96; weaknesses
    of, 24, 25–26, 68–69, 96
Man Who Died Twice, The, 64
"Many Are Called," 140
Marvell, Andrew, 43
"Master, The," 32
Masters, Edgar Lee, 10, 19–20, 148
Matthias at the Door, 63

"Maya," 32, 37–38

Melville, Herman, 3, 19, 99, 117

Merlin: Arthur's role in, 104–5, 108–9; characterization in, 108, 113; despair and grief as themes in, 94, 105; general themes in, 105, 108–9; as major work, 7–8, 32, 62, 113, 125; Merlin's role in, 43, 52, 101, 102, 105–6, 108–11, 112–13, 125; structure of, 94, 95; style of, 1, 97, 111–13; Vivian's role in, 30, 106–8, 109, 110, 112, 113; weaknesses of, 7, 27, 92, 94, 125

Midsummer Night's Dream, A (Shakespeare), 35

Mifflin, Lloyd, 15

"Mill, The," 32

"Miniver Cheevy": autobiographical elements in, 91–92, 93, 94–95; characterization in, 91–93, 120, 144; as major work, 9, 31, 32, 94

"Mr. Edwards and the Spider" (Lowell), 49–52

"Mr. Flood's Party," 19, 32, 91, 145–47

"Modernities," 132

"Monadnock" (Emerson), 80, 81, 89–90

"Monadnok through the Trees," 89–90

"Monocle de Mon Oncle, Le" (Stevens), 11

Moody, William Vaughn: as poet, 15, 127, 139, 140–41; Robinson compared to, 134, 142

Moore, Marianne, 11

Moore, Merrill, 140

Morte D'Arthur, Le (Malory), 102

"Mortmain," 32, 60

"Most of It, The" (Frost), 122

Moulton, Louise Chandler, 15

"My Secret" (Tabb), 141

"New England," 32, 38–39, 144

"New Year's Day" (Lowell), 48

Nicodemus, 94, 95

"Octaves": general themes in, 82, 83; style of, 7, 10–11, 83, 131

"Ode in Time of Hesitation" (Moody), 139

"Old Cumberland Beggar, The" (Wordsworth), 53

"Old King Cole," 23

"Old Man's Winter Night, An" (Frost), 7, 122

"Old Trails," 23

"Our Lady of Walsingham" (Lowell), 48–49

"Oversoul, The" (Emerson), 76, 77

Pattee, Fred, 138, 141

"Pity of the Leaves, The," 122, 131

Plato, 6

Poe, Edgar Allan, 11, 14, 134

"Poet, The" (Emerson), 3, 79–80

Poets of America (Stedman), 14–15

"Poor Relation, The," 32, 35–36, 123

Porcupine, The, 95, 96

Pound, Ezra, 11, 142

"Power" (Emerson), 1, 2

Praed, Winthrop Mackworth, 62

Prophetiae Merlini (Geoffrey of Monmouth), 111

Ransom, John Crowe, 31

Redman, Ben Ray, 134

Reese, Lizette Woodworth, 15

Region of the Summer Stars, The (C. Williams), 103, 104

"Rembrandt to Rembrandt," 124, 133, 134, 148

"Reuben Bright," 32, 120, 143–44

"Richard Cory," 32, 120, 141–42

Riley, James Whitcomb, 15, 139

Rilke, Rainer Maria, 144

Robinson, Dean (brother), 75

Robinson, Edward (father), 75, 117

Robinson, Edwin Arlington: background of, 56, 59, 64–65, 70, 73–74, 75–76, 80–81, 82, 91, 92, 93, 108, 115, 116, 117–18, 134, 139–40; and Browning, 2, 9, 62, 132; Bunyan's influence on, 23; Carlyle's influence on, 75, 76; and Coleridge, 127, 132; Crabbe compared to, 142, 153; death of, 117,

137; Dickinson compared to, 73–74, 100; and Eliot, 11, 95, 96, 116; and Emerson, 1, 2, 3, 20, 26, 27, 75, 76–78, 79–82, 83, 84–85, 86, 88, 89, 91, 93, 95, 96, 97, 98–99, 100, 118; and Frost, 1, 3, 7, 9, 89, 90, 91, 94, 100, 122, 123, 125, 133, 135, 137, 144, 148; Hardy compared to, 2, 37, 52–53, 57, 62, 123, 142, 145, 153; and Hawthorne, 97, 98, 99–100, 117–18, 122; idealism of, 76, 98, 100; as influential writer, 10, 11, 95, 96, 122; James's (William) influence on, 75, 77; letters of, 2, 75, 76, 77, 78, 80–81, 84, 89, 96; Longfellow's influence on, 2; and Lowell, 46, 122; materialism as viewed by, 74–75, 78; Melville compared to, 3, 117; Moody compared to, 134, 142; philosophy of, 6, 59, 91, 93, 96, 111, 119, 134–35; as poet, 4, 6, 15–16, 19, 23–24, 27, 28, 61, 71, 98, 119, 121, 125, 133–35, 142–43, 148, 153; as realist, 111–12, 135; religion as viewed by, 76, 95, 98, 119; as romantic, 111, 127, 135; science as viewed by, 78–79, 98; Spencer's influence on, 74, 75, 76, 77; and Stevens, 11, 134; Tennyson's influence on, 2, 149; and Whitman, 20, 25, 26, 84, 135; and Wordsworth, 61, 62, 149; Yeats compared to, 29–30, 132
Robinson, Edwin Arlington, works of: blank verse, 7–8; characterization in, 17–18, 19, 22, 23, 35, 58, 59–60, 62, 63, 64, 91, 112, 120, 121, 144–45, 148, 153; communication as theme in, 17–18, 19; compassion and pity in, 65, 91; conjecture in, 58, 59, 60, 67, 70, 71; death as theme in, 65, 145; despair and grief as themes in, 35, 65, 69, 89, 105, 142, 143; as dramas, 20, 58, 60, 61, 64, 119, 122; failure as theme in, 64, 105, 116–17; fate as theme in, 2, 62, 145; general themes in, 18, 22, 30, 64, 65, 70,

71, 116, 145; history in, 58, 120; humor in, 65, 69, 70, 91, 148; irony in, 31, 55, 64, 65, 69, 122, 133, 145; isolation and loneliness as themes in, 63, 116–17, 119, 144–45, 148; language in, 20, 68, 127, 130, 132–33, 134, 135; mood of, 69, 89, 127, 130; myth in, 16, 27, 52; passion vs. reason as theme in, 37, 45, 46, 52; past vs. present as theme in, 64, 65; reader's role in, 20, 59, 61, 70; rhymed verse, 7, 8–9, 10–11; satire in, 61, 65, 144; sensibility of, 58–59, 91; setting of, 17, 19, 20, 62–63, 71, 119–20, 142; sincerity of, 67, 123; structure of, 122, 127; style of, 6–7, 16, 19, 20, 27, 55, 58, 60–61, 62, 64, 65, 67–68, 71, 89, 118, 121–22, 127, 145; weaknesses of, 11, 16, 24, 26, 29–32, 56, 57, 61, 62, 64, 100, 115, 121, 138, 140. *See also specific volumes and poems*
Robinson, Emma (sister-in-law), 91
Robinson, Mary Palmer (mother), 75, 76, 80, 81
Roman Bartholow, 27
Roosevelt, Theodore, 117, 140
Rossetti, Dante Gabriel, 62
Royce, Josiah, 75
Russell, George, 31

"Sage, The," Emerson as viewed in, 1, 2, 84, 85, 98–99
Sandburg, Carl, 11, 148
Santayana, George, 15
Sartor Resartus (Carlyle), 75
"Self-Reliance" (Emerson), 77
Shafer, Robert, 141
"Sheaves, The," 32
Sill, Edward, 127, 134
"Sinners in the Hands of an Angry God" (Edwards), 49, 51
"Socrates" (Winters), 45
"Souvenir," 32
Spencer, Herbert, 86; literary influence on Robinson of, 74, 75, 76, 77
Spoon River Anthology (Masters), 10

"Spring Pools" (Frost), 122
Stedman, Edmund, 14–15
Sterling, George, 127, 134
Stevens, Wallace: as poet, 6, 41, 121;
    and Robinson, 11, 134
Stickney, Trumbull, 15, 139, 140–41,
    142
Stoddard, Elizabeth, 15
"Story of the Ashes and the Flame,
    The," 130
Sullivan, Harry Stack, 70
"Supremacy," 131
Swinburne, Algernon Charles, 127

Tabb, John Bannister, 15, 141
Taliessin through Logres (C. Williams),
    103, 104
Tennyson, Alfred, 2, 149
That Hideous Strength (Lewis), 103–4
Thaxter, Celia, 138
Thomas, Edith Matilda, 15
"Thomas Hood," 77
Thoreau, Henry David, 27
"Three Quatrains," 130
Three Taverns, The, 9
"Three Taverns, The," 94, 124
Torrent and the Night Before, The, 1,
    140; style of, 77, 79, 91
"To Speak of the Woe that is in Mar-
    riage" (Lowell), 46
"To What Strangers? What Welcome?"
    (Cunningham), 42, 43–45
*Town down the River, The. See specific
    poems*
"Trembling of the Veil, The" (Yeats),
    49
Tristram: general themes in, 52, 94; Is-
    olt's role in, 39–40, 52; language
    in, 132, 134; as major work, 32,
    56, 117; structure of, 94, 95; style
    of, 97, 112; weaknesses of, 27, 31,
    92, 94
Turberville, George, 145
"Two Sonnets," 80, 81

"Unforgiven, The," 32, 33–35
"Upon a Dying Lady" (Yeats), 29–30
"Uriel" (Emerson), 78, 86

Van Dyke, Henry, 15
Van Zorn, 95–96
"Verlaine," 77, 131
Very, Jones, 3
"Veteran Sirens," 32, 33
Vita Merlini (Geoffrey of Monmouth),
    101, 103, 111

Waller, Edmund, 128, 129
"Walt Whitman," 1, 16–17, 77, 83–
    84
"Wandering Jew, The," 28, 31, 116,
    148
Warton, Joseph, 129
Whitman, Walt: as poet, 6, 11, 14, 20,
    25, 121; and Robinson, 20, 25,
    26, 84, 135. *See also specific
    poems*
Wilde, Oscar, 127
Williams, Charles, 103. *See also specific
    poems*
Williams, William Carlos, 134
Winters, Yvor, 1, 2, 3, 115–16. *See also
    specific poems*
Wordsworth, William, 61, 62, 149
Wright, James, 122

Yeats, William Butler: as poet, 11, 49,
    123, 127; Robinson compared to,
    29–30, 132. *See also specific
    poems*

Zabel, Morton Dauwen, 62
Ziff, Larzer, 140
"Zola," 77, 79, 130

Modern Critical Views

Continued from front of book

Gabriel García Márquez
Andrew Marvell
Carson McCullers
Herman Melville
George Meredith
James Merrill
John Stuart Mill
Arthur Miller
Henry Miller
John Milton
Yukio Mishima
Molière
Michel de Montaigne
Eugenio Montale
Marianne Moore
Alberto Moravia
Toni Morrison
Alice Munro
Iris Murdoch
Robert Musil
Vladimir Nabokov
V. S. Naipaul
R. K. Narayan
Pablo Neruda
John Henry, Cardinal
  Newman
Friedrich Nietzsche
Frank Norris
Joyce Carol Oates
Sean O'Casey
Flannery O'Connor
Christopher Okigbo
Charles Olson
Eugene O'Neill
José Ortega y Gasset
Joe Orton
George Orwell
Ovid
Wilfred Owen
Amos Oz
Cynthia Ozick
Grace Paley
Blaise Pascal
Walter Pater
Octavio Paz
Walker Percy
Petrarch
Pindar
Harold Pinter
Luigi Pirandello
Sylvia Plath
Plato

Plautus
Edgar Allan Poe
Poets of Sensibility & the
  Sublime
Poets of the Nineties
Alexander Pope
Katherine Anne Porter
Ezra Pound
Anthony Powell
Pre-Raphaelite Poets
Marcel Proust
Manuel Puig
Alexander Pushkin
Thomas Pynchon
Francisco de Quevedo
François Rabelais
Jean Racine
Ishmael Reed
Adrienne Rich
Samuel Richardson
Mordecai Richler
Rainer Maria Rilke
Arthur Rimbaud
Edwin Arlington Robinson
Theodore Roethke
Philip Roth
Jean-Jacques Rousseau
John Ruskin
J. D. Salinger
Jean-Paul Sartre
Gershom Scholem
Sir Walter Scott
William Shakespeare
  (3 vols.)
  Histories & Poems
  Comedies & Romances
  Tragedies
George Bernard Shaw
Mary Wollstonecraft
  Shelley
Percy Bysshe Shelley
Sam Shepard
Richard Brinsley Sheridan
Sir Philip Sidney
Isaac Bashevis Singer
Tobias Smollett
Alexander Solzhenitsyn
Sophocles
Wole Soyinka
Edmund Spenser
Gertrude Stein
John Steinbeck

Stendhal
Laurence Sterne
Wallace Stevens
Robert Louis Stevenson
Tom Stoppard
August Strindberg
Jonathan Swift
John Millington Synge
Alfred, Lord Tennyson
William Makepeace
  Thackeray
Dylan Thomas
Henry David Thoreau
James Thurber and S. J.
  Perelman
J. R. R. Tolkien
Leo Tolstoy
Jean Toomer
Lionel Trilling
Anthony Trollope
Ivan Turgenev
Mark Twain
Miguel de Unamuno
John Updike
Paul Valéry
Cesar Vallejo
Lope de Vega
Gore Vidal
Virgil
Voltaire
Kurt Vonnegut
Derek Walcott
Alice Walker
Robert Penn Warren
Evelyn Waugh
H. G. Wells
Eudora Welty
Nathanael West
Edith Wharton
Patrick White
Walt Whitman
Oscar Wilde
Tennessee Williams
William Carlos Williams
Thomas Wolfe
Virginia Woolf
William Wordsworth
Jay Wright
Richard Wright
William Butler Yeats
A. B. Yehoshua
Emile Zola

DATE DUE

DEMCO 38-297